PREACH
AND
HEAL

*What does Jesus expect
His Church to do?*

JOHN HUGGETT

AuthorHouse™ UK
1663 Liberty Drive
Bloomington, IN 47403 USA
www.authorhouse.co.uk
Phone: UK TFN: 0800 0148641 (Toll Free inside the UK)
        UK Local: 02036 956322 (+44 20 3695 6322 from outside the UK)

Published by AuthorHouse   09/07/2021

ISBN: 978-1-6655-9033-4 (sc)
ISBN: 978-1-6655-9032-7 (hc)
ISBN: 978-1-6655-9034-1 (e)

Library of Congress Control Number: 2021917498

Print information available on the last page.

Paraphrases by the author

This book is printed on acid-free paper.

DEDICATION

Dedicated to my wonderful wife Chris,
my faithful long-term partner in life
and in the healing ministry, who constantly
expresses the love and power of Jesus.

ACKNOWLEDGMENTS

In chapter 8 some instances of raising the dead are summarised with grateful thanks from *The dead are raised up* by the Reverend F L Wyman (Ken-Pax Publishing Co. Ltd, 1954) and from *Come, Holy Spirit* by Bishop David Pytches (Hodder and Stoughton, 1985).

I extend my warm appreciation to all who have contributed in any way to *Preach and Heal*, especially

Christine Huggett
The Reverend Doctor Andrew Daunton-Fear
The Reverend Chris Oldroyd
Doctor Andrew Gibson
The Reverend Trevor Dearing
Mervyn Brown
Paul Huggett
Debra Sencil
Philip Clarkson
Will Bartola

Together with my sponsors, editors, printers and distributors and all the teams at Authorhouse.

God bless you all!

CONTENTS

Come this way to explore anew what
Jesus Christ can do through you

Plus over 300 Bible References

THE KEY BIBLE REFERENCES

The Outreach Commands of Jesus

Go into all the world and preach the good news to all creation. (Mark 16:15)

As you go, preach this message: "The Kingdom of Heaven is near." Heal the sick. Raise the dead. Cleanse the lepers. Drive out demons. Freely you have received, freely give. (Matthew 10:7–8)

His Promise of Greater Things

Truly, truly I tell you, anyone who has faith in Me will do the works that I've been doing. He will do even greater things than these, because I'm going to the Father. (John 14:12)

How Can We Do the Works That Jesus Did?

You will receive dynamite power when the Holy Spirit comes upon you. (Acts 1:8; "dynamite power" = *dunamis*)

TEN DYNAMIC DISCOVERIES

Did you know that ...?

- Jesus never sent out anyone to preach the Gospel message without also telling them to heal the sick and cast out demons, *in His Name* (with His authority) *and in the power of His Spirit* (released through their mouths and hands).
- Jesus doesn't say to us, "You do the preaching and I'll do the healing." He expects us to do both, *in His Name and in the power of His Spirit* (and He's put no sell-by date on this).
- Apart from what we say in the creeds, such as "born of the virgin Mary" and "suffered under Pontius Pilate", there's nothing that Jesus did while on earth in body that we believers cannot do, *in His Name and in the power of His Spirit*.
- At the turn of the millennium, the fastest-growing churches in the world were ones that worked signs and wonders—healings and miracles—*in His Name and in the power of His Spirit*.
- The Church that witnesses by using lips and lives but without signs and wonders is using only two-thirds of the equipment that God has provided.
- If we remove the supernatural from the Bible, we'll only have half a Bible left! The Old Testament is shot through with the supernatural. So are the Gospels, the Acts, and the book of Revelation. And there are about sixty references to it in the Epistles.
- Jesus did not come to earth and die just to save souls but to save sinners—that is, to make them whole.
- After the Day of Pentecost, every time the Bible says that someone was filled with the Holy Spirit, they immediately opened their mouth and spoke.

- During the twentieth century many people were raised from the dead.
- Among God's ultimate loving purposes, He wants us to be holy, He wants us whole, and He wants us healing!

CHAPTER 1

The Background to Greater Things

Between the 1960s and the middle of the 1990s millions of Christians and thousands of churches all over the world enjoyed a period of spiritual renewal. Many of us experienced fresh awakenings, learned deeper scriptural truths, and witnessed powerful manifestations of the Holy Spirit. The Charismatic Renewal emphasised the power of the Spirit (Luke 24:49 and Acts 1:8) and His supernatural gifts—such as prophecy, healing, and miracles (1 Corinthians 12:8-10)—as available to every Christian believer (1 Corinthians 14:1). These had already been rediscovered by the Pentecostals earlier in that century, but in the seventies they became a feature of every major denomination. *Charismata* means "gifts of grace".

Therefore I am writing this not only as an Evangelical Anglican who emphasises the Bible, the Cross, and the Gospel, but as a Charismatic Christian who emphasises the Spirit, His power, and His wonders—for the Bible has plenty to say about every one of these.

Tremendous Encouragements

By 1980 all the biblical miracles had been paralleled somewhere in the world, particularly during spiritual revivals in parts of Africa, Asia, and South America. Throughout the eighties the number of Christians in the continent of Africa mushroomed from 70 million to a remarkable 250 million. In the nineties more people worldwide became Christians, and more claimed to be healed through Christian ministry,

1

than throughout the whole of history. By the end of the millennium the fastest-growing churches in the world were the ones working signs and wonders—healings and miracles—in the Name of Jesus and in the power of His Spirit. It was an exciting time to be living in!

Conscious Experience

By the year 2000 people calling themselves Christians numbered two billion. A quarter were Pentecostal or Charismatic, the largest grouping after the Roman Catholics. Of these, eleven million said they had experienced the Baptism in the Holy Spirit (Matthew 3:11 and Acts 1:5), a definite, conscious, visible filling with the Spirit by Jesus Christ. This tends to be a dynamic and liberating experience that happens only once and is unforgettable. It's sometimes called by a variety of other names, but basically it's a "Personal Pentecost".

These Spirit-filled believers included over half of all Evangelical Christians in the world, plus hundreds of thousands of people from other Christian traditions: Pentecostal, Protestant, Catholic, Anglican, Lutheran, Orthodox, Coptic, Independent, and others. All over the world the Spirit was moving in manifest ways, as well as many quiet ways.

Filled with the Holy Spirit we did not become better Christians, nor were we automatically better than other people, but each of us was better empowered and better equipped.

Visible Evidence

Most of us manifested this experience of the Spirit first by speaking in tongues—languages we had not learned (Acts 19:6). Others had other verbal gifts of the Holy Spirit, such as prophecy (words given directly from God) or the word of knowledge (a message for others of supernatural knowledge). Many people also had an emotional release, in tears, or laughter.

The Charismatic experience proved an incentive and motivation for each of us to achieve more for Christ than we otherwise would have done. However, we realised that we needed frequently to be filled with the Holy Spirit. The *Dictionary of Theology* makes this very clear: "The Pentecostal experience is not a goal to be reached, nor a place to stand, but a door to a fuller and deeper life in the Holy Spirit."

Frequent Consequences

Many people renewed in the Spirit found their spiritual vision widening. Others described how things they'd seen in black and white (both in the Bible and elsewhere) they now viewed in Technicolour. Again and again such people described the same frequent results:

- a deeper awareness of the presence of Jesus
- a greater expectancy of what He will do
- a penetrating entry into the supernatural realm
- a clearer understanding of the voice of God
- a deeper understanding of the Holy Scriptures
- boldness in testifying about our relationship with Jesus
- greater liberty in praise and worship
- treasuring our inheritance as adopted children of God the Father
- openness to whatever the Holy Spirit wants to do
- seeking and using the power and gifts of the Spirit
- insight into the reality of evil forces and Jesus' victory over them
- using Christ's authority (*exousia*) to command blessing and rebuke evil
- more effective ministry for the Lord
- doing the works of Jesus—signs and wonders

Wakeup Call

The Charismatic Renewal not only ignited the use of the power and gifts of the Spirit, but it provided a wakeup call to churches here and abroad in connection with many other things:

New styles of praise and worship

These were ushered in apart from, alongside, and within familiar structures, using all kinds of musical instruments (as in Psalm 150), as well as the organ. Song writers like Graham Kendrick made a major contribution to the Charismatic Movement. The new hymns, songs, and choruses were often ones of adoration, so, as well as thanking God for what He had done for us, we exalted Him for who He is. Some of us could not lift Him high enough, so at appropriate points of praise during the worship we *raised* our hands, like the Jews of old. We also *clapped* hands, not only as an accompaniment to some of the songs or for applause but as a "clap offering" to the Lord. Sometimes too we *joined* hands with people next to us, especially during fellowship songs and when we all prayed the Grace together. We found as well that not only could we praise God for particular circumstances but that our praise could help *change* circumstances! Sometimes the worship was spontaneous, as were aids to it, such as dancing, flag-waving, and laughter!

New kinds of prayer and ministry

Soon some prayer meetings became *praise* and prayer meetings, first uplifting the Lord and waiting upon Him in case He should speak to us. Prayer ministry for the needs of individuals was at the heart of the renewal, usually accompanied by the laying-on-of-hands. For deeper needs, trained Christians offered prayer counselling. Extempore prayer became a feature of a number of non-Evangelical churches. We discovered as well that previously unfamiliar types of prayer could be powerful and effective, such as the prayer of faith and expectancy (Mark 11:24), the prayer of command and authority (Acts 3:6), two-in-agreement (Matthew 18:19—usually joining hands) and two-way prayer—when for instance we might ask the Lord to guide us about a particular situation and then listen for His answers (cf. Acts 16:6–10).

New forms of church and arrangements

"Every member ministry" was encouraged, and turning congregations (that meet together) into fellowships (that share together). Many new churches were planted, and several new Christian communities were established. It was the era of the small group. This was where many people first manifested spiritual gifts and ministered to one another, often when their churches were "not ready" for these things in the main services. Some larger churches decided to split into cell groups. It was also the era of the big meetings and the "big speakers". People often travelled many miles to the large Charismatic rallies. John Wimber's Vineyard Movement made a real impact here in the UK, and large annual conferences attracted many, such as Bishop David Pytches' New Wine. Meanwhile, at Holy Trinity Church, Brompton, London, a new, popular, introductory course was launched, and was soon flourishing right across the globe: Nicky Gumbel's Alpha.

Breath Ministries

My wife Christine and I were especially inspired by a mini-revival at St Paul's Church, Hainault, Essex, where the Rev Trevor Dearing was the vicar. After I had served twelve years as a parish priest, we founded Breath Fellowship Trust, an interdenominational charity which, over forty years, took us to three hundred venues in the UK and to several other countries.

Our Praise, Healing and Renewal rallies always consisted of "The Worship, the Word and the Wonders". It was said that anything could happen at these meetings, and often did! A number of regulars could not wait to get there. As a result of all these gatherings, hundreds of people were saved, healed, delivered, changed, and filled with the Holy Spirit.

At our training days and residential conferences in England and Wales, I trained clergy and others in how to teach about and give prayer ministry for all areas of Christian healing and wholeness. Consequently, churches began holding healing prayer services, healing prayer groups sprang up in several different areas, and some doctors and therapists incorporated lessons learned into their work.

In our books and recordings sent worldwide, we taught biblical principles, told of some exciting things the Lord had been doing, and attempted to answer enquirers' frequently asked questions.

Others' Reactions

Many other Christians and churches worldwide did not participate in the renewal. Many clergy who did not agree with some aspects of Charismatic theology and practice simply ignored the movement, and a few actively opposed us—though some had to think what to do about such things when their children were filled with the Spirit at college or summer camp! Some other brothers and sisters opened their church doors to Charismatic speakers when they learned what a difference these had made to their own church members.

Eventually many other church leaders—wisely, I think—took what they regarded as helpful in the ongoing renewal and began to incorporate this into their own church programmes, especially the new worship songs, the prayer ministry, and often the healing prayer services.

But Satan was very active in attempting to spoil what was happening, and he sometimes succeeded. The opposition by some leaders increased. There were also misunderstandings, disputes, and division. Occasionally there were abuses, extremes, and scandals. But overall the thirty-year-plus renewal remained Bible based, glorifying to the Lord, *and* Christ centred. And, as far as I know, there was never any suggestion of a Holy Spirit faith contrasted with a Son of God faith. For Jesus once said of the Holy Spirit, "He shall glorify Me" (John 16:14), and the more we moved in the Spirit the more we wanted to love, worship, and please our Saviour and Lord.

Black Embers

Thirty years on, and the church situation in the UK is very different. This country is becoming increasingly secular, Christianity is being marginalised, and worshippers in established churches are dwindling—though, once the Covid-19 virus arrived, there were millions of new viewers of church services online. There are also different attitudes, different atmospheres, and different activities in comparison to the period of renewal.

A few years ago, my wife Chris remarked to Canon Michael Green, the former principal of an Evangelical theological college, "The fire's died down, hasn't it?"

His reply was immediate: "The embers have turned black."

This may sound strange to the younger generation, or to those the renewal passed by, especially if they belong to a church (and there are still many) which is vibrant and growing and which is even planting new churches, but God has so much more to give to His children!

For a start, there are the blessings I've already listed and which have been experienced so much by people filled with the Spirit. And He has so much more for us to do for Him, including those outreach opportunities, and—yes—even greater things than these!

Limited Service

Catholics stress the Church that God desires,
Liberals stress the virtues He admires,
Evangelicals the faith which He requires,
Charismatics the works that He inspires.
In all of these when shall we see
The greater things He said would be?

(Author's assessment)

Outreach Commands

Among the things which were taken seriously during the renewal but are now adhered to less are those outreach commands (Mark 16:15 and Matthew 10:7–8). Some of these are needed to be obeyed only occasionally, but the first two are for all times: *preach* and *heal*, for Jesus wants Christians constantly to preach the Gospel to unbelievers, as there are always lost sinners around us. He also wants us to heal the sick, as those in need are always around us.

We may no longer be living in a period of spiritual renewal, but that does not mean that God is any less willing to bless and use us just as much. It seems that many Christians are unintentionally not giving God the Holy Spirit liberty to do all that He desires to do. He is waiting for more believers and churches to use His dynamite power for this. I believe that, if we faithfully obey the outreach commands of Christ, we shall not only see more people won to Him but be blessed even more ourselves. That's one of the lessons that the renewal teaches us.

So come with me now as we explore together these commands: what they are, what they mean, and how we can put them into practice. Let's go!

CHAPTER 2

The Outreach Commands of Christ

The Lord Jesus Christ is the Creator of the Universe (John 1:3), the Saviour of the World (John 4:42), and the Head of the Church (Colossians 1:18). He became all three in that order. The Church is the worldwide body of Christian believers who worship God and who seek to love, serve, and obey Him. With these things in mind, I invite you to investigate with me the following *big questions*.

Big Questions

- Before this universe was created, what did Almighty God plan for only His Church to do?
- After God's Son came to earth as Jesus Christ, what did He train only His disciples to do?
- After Jesus rose again and before He ascended, what did He tell only His followers to do?
- Now He is back upon His heavenly throne, what is He expecting only His Church to do?

Big Answers

As far as outreach is concerned, the answers to all these four questions are exactly the same:

Preach the Gospel—the good news that the Kingdom of God is available through Christ.

Heal the sick—in spirit, soul (mind, will, emotions), body, relationships, and circumstances.

Cleanse the lepers—go to the "outcasts"—also to the people most seriously ill.

Cast out demons—evil spirits possessing or oppressing an individual.

Raise the dead—if led to by the Holy Spirit.

Freely give—share with those who need them the gifts and talents that God has given to you.

Note: This does not mean that every Christian should be doing all these things all of the time! But here's something else that challenged us in the renewal: *Jesus never sent anyone out to preach the Gospel message without telling them also to heal the sick and cast out demons.*

And the astonishing fact is that, apart from the things we say in the creeds, such as "born of the virgin Mary" and "suffered under Pontius Pilate", there's nothing Jesus did while He was here on earth in body that we cannot do too, in His Name and in the power of His Holy Spirit.

Great Commission

In the Epilogue to Mark's Gospel (author unknown) the great commission of Mark 16:15 has been the subject of many a missionary sermon. It's led thousands to go to different mission fields and some to lay down their lives: "Go into all the world and preach the good news to all creation." We shall look at this later, but notice the precious promises in the same context:

> "These signs will accompany those who believe: In My Name they will drive out demons … They will place their hands on sick people, and they will get well" (Mark 16:17–18).

The parallel passage in Matthew 28:19–20 reads,

> Go and make disciples of all nations, baptising them into the Name of the Father and of the Son and of the Holy Spirit, and teaching them to obey *everything I have commanded you.* (Italics mine.)

So it's time to ask: *What* did he command them? What particular instructions did he give His disciples?

Different Commands

There were three main types of orders that Christ gave to His disciples during His ministry: general commands, fellowship commands, and outreach commands.

General commands were those which Jesus announced to the multitudes: "Love your God", "Love your neighbours" (Luke 10:27), and "Love your enemies" (Matthew 5:44).

Fellowship commands were those to be obeyed by the disciples just among themselves: "Abide in Me and I will in you" (John 15:4), "Do this in remembrance of Me" (Luke 22:19), and His new commandment: "Love one another as I have loved you" (John 13:34).

Outreach commands are what we are exploring here. They are all just as important today as they were when they were given.

Irrelevant Instructions?

Many Christians in the twenty-first century ignore the Lord's outreach commands in Matthew 10. Some do not realise they are there, others are not bothered to consider them, and some that do so in the

UK have decided that they were only relevant for 2,000 years ago and 2,000 miles away. They argue that Jesus intended them only for His disciples' mission to the Jews, not our mission to the world. They also point out the reference to leprosy, and say that this disease is not as big an issue these days as it was in that time and place. Other Christians miss the aim of wholeness. They say, "We have doctors and hospitals. Why do we need anything else?" Still others ignore making use of supernatural ministries, such as healing and deliverance. This may be due to ignorance, apathy, unbelief, pride, jealousy, or fear, but often it appears to be because they have never seen a miracle. What a difference it can make when they do!

Good Reasons

In spite of these reservations some have, I believe there are still good reasons to obey the outreach commands of Christ. After all, the proof of the pudding is in the eating!

- The early Church fathers in the first centuries AD obviously believed that Christ intended them to continue to do His supernatural works, and they discovered that they were able to.
- Many signs and wonders occurred during spiritual revivals, often because some believers were prepared to trust the Lord for them. As a result, many unbelievers were converted.
- During the twentieth century, Pentecostals and Charismatics found that practising these commands brought fruitful results, in some cases transforming whole communities.

Training Stages

From the start of His earthly ministry Jesus was training His disciples to be missionaries: "Follow Me, and I will make you fishers of men" (Matthew 4:19). He probably trained them in the same way that other rabbis (teachers) did in those days—in three stages, possibly corresponding to each of the three years of His ministry.

In the first stage those disciples listened to what He said and observed what He did. In the second stage they still did this but probably also assisted Him in practical ways, such as baptising people in the River Jordan. In the third stage He sent them all out, *on their own*, with His power and authority, to speak His words and to do His mighty works.

It was before they went that time that Jesus gave them His outreach commands (Matthew 10:7–8). He was simply summarising what He'd trained them to do. It was His permanent outreach policy.

When He later sent the seventy (or seventy-two) "lay people", they were instructed to do the same things (Luke 10:1). Their message came first, but they were also to heal the sick, and rejoiced when demons departed when commanded to in His Name. Then He promised that future believers in Him would do these things too (John 14:12). They continued faithfully to do them, and His later disciples followed the same outreach policy.

All this threatened to end when Jesus was crucified, but God acted on two particular days to ensure it did not: Easter, when Christ rose from the dead, and Pentecost, when the Holy Spirit came.

CHAPTER 3

The Church's Varied Responses

I t all started well: 120 believers were consciously filled with the Holy Spirit and praised the Lord in tongues (Acts 2:4). On that occasion these were understood by everyone around. Peter the fisherman preached from the Bible how in the last days (that's now), ordinary people would be doing extraordinary things (Joel 2:28–29 and Acts 2:17–18). Then Peter preached from his own experience of how Jesus was crucified, rose from the dead, and was the promised Messiah (Christ). As a result of this anointed sermon 3,000 other people were converted and baptised. This later increased to 5,000.

While establishing the Church, the disciples (now called apostles— "sent ones") still found time to work signs and wonders—healings and miracles, testimonies to the risen life and power of Christ. Later, both Peter and Paul preached, healed, dealt with demons, and raised the dead. But ordinary Christians also brought healing, such as Ananias, and preached, such as Apollos (Acts 9:17–19 and Acts 18:24–28). Ordinary people were doing extraordinary things.

Powerful Acts

"The Acts of the Holy Spirit", as some call the book, is therefore filled with frequent miracles and persecuted believers. It was all written by St Luke, St Paul's personal friend and physician (probably a herbalist), who first joined Paul on his second missionary journey at Troas. Doctor Luke was an accurate reporter and historian, and he was another follower of "Doctor Jesus". Luke starts off by referring back to his own written Gospel, where he had told about what Jesus *began* to do and teach (His works and His words). For His work of redemption had finished on Calvary, but His work of salvation (making people whole) would continue, with His Holy Spirit first acting through the early Church. And Luke's account of that is exciting!

The main theme of the book of Acts, preaching the Gospel, is referred to no less than twenty-six times, for within the space of thirty years Christian churches had sprung up all around the Mediterranean Sea, from Jerusalem to Rome.

Next, as one might expect, comes healing the sick, which is mentioned ten times. In addition, there would certainly be more healings among the eight references to signs and wonders.

There is no mention of leprosy, probably because the Church was soon on the move, and leprosy was not such a big issue everywhere they went. But the early Church did not fail to go to the outcasts—a favourite theme of St Luke's Gospel—or to reach out to the seriously ill.

There are four references to dealing with demons and two to raising the dead.

Many in the Christian Church faithfully continued to obey the outreach commands of the Lord, and to use the spiritual gifts to aid them in this ministry, for at least five centuries after Christ's ascension into Heaven. My friend Rev Doctor Andrew Daunton-Fear has researched the healing ministry among the early Church fathers. He found there are various instances of healing and deliverance.

Irenaeus, a bishop in the second century, shared a remarkable observation: "None who believe in Christ and call upon His Name remain unhealed."

St Augustine, in the fourth century, said, "We see there are many miracles at this day wrought by God."

Centuries Between

Early in the fourth century Constantine became the Holy Roman Emperor and eventually was baptised as a Christian. Christianity became the official religion of the empire, and citizens tended to think of themselves as belonging to the Church, so thousands who had no genuine faith began calling themselves Christians. Thus fewer people had the simple faith required to expect miraculous healings or the other things Jesus was expecting His Church to provide.

During the monastic life of the Dark Ages and Middle Ages, suffering was hailed as a virtue, and to bear sickness stoically was praised. The ministry of healing never died out completely, and there are countless instances of individual saints working miracles—though some of these are legends, or were mixed with superstition.

But for over 1,500 years the prevailing attitude to sickness and disease was to be a fatalistic one (such as Islam now teaches), and these things were regarded as God's judgement upon people. Though Christians played leading parts in the foundation of hospitals and orphanages, there was no extensive attempt to practise or encourage a healing ministry through positive specific prayer and ministry.

Missionary Movements

The Reformation of the sixteenth century especially brought the availability of the Bible, the return of the doctrine of justification by faith, and consequently fresh drives to spread the Gospel through Europe and beyond. These things would eventually lead to the success of the Evangelical Revival in this country in the eighteenth century, then to the great missionary movements of the nineteenth century, and ultimately to the globalisation of Evangelism through churches, missions, and advanced technology in the twentieth century.

The nineteenth century also saw much increase in social care and aiding the poor. Eventually there followed the consequent proliferation of charities, Christian and otherwise.

Healing Advances

After the Reformation, fresh attempts were made to revive the healing ministry. Martin Luther in the sixteenth century was one of those who rediscovered the Lord's outreach commands, and he

15

announced, "It still does happen that by calling on His Name the sick are healed."

Count Zinzendorf, in the eighteenth century, declared, "I testify that apostolic powers are manifested. We now have undeniable proof of the healing of incurable maladies by prayer."

William Booth, in the nineteenth century, wrote, "The recent remarkable signs and wonders wrought among us demand our consideration. I believe in the necessity of these gifts."

When there has been a genuine spiritual revival there has often been a resurgence of the same things. John Wesley recorded 200 cases of divine healing in his famous journal.

As we have seen, however, it's only since the start of the twentieth century, following the Azusa Street revival in the USA, that Pentecostals have made healing a regular part of their church programmes. During the decades that followed, wonderful miracles were performed by men of God like John G Lake of the USA and Smith Wigglesworth of the UK.

Around that time some Anglicans became heavily involved with divine healing. James Moore Hickson, encouraged by some bishops, exercised a worldwide healing ministry. Soon in the UK there were several healing homes, healing guilds, healing missions, healing evangelists, and occasional healing services. But none of these was widely known about.

Supernatural Ministries

From the 1960s the Charismatic Renewal brought a welcome return to the acts of the New Testament, as, for the first time since the fifth century, the outreach commands of Jesus were taken seriously and practised by a substantial proportion of the universal Church, with Christians of all kinds ministering to one another and to others in need.

Besides the evangelistic campaigns, the big meetings, and the small groups, there were many new ministries, both inter-church and denominational—for renewal, outreach, prophecy, physical and inner healing, listening and prayer counselling, deliverance, relationships, teaching and training, music and worship, and combined ministries.

Changing Times

The widespread continuous Charismatic Renewal came to an end somewhere in the nineties, after a "time of refreshing" among some churches of the West. Many UK churches were then "into renewal", which meant that they'd embraced some Charismatic activities. But often you could share spiritual gifts only in the small groups or prayer ministry. Actual signs and wonders were found more in the specifically Charismatic gatherings (words of knowledge were frequent), in the large evangelistic campaigns, and in the Pentecostal and new churches.

By 1990, in many UK towns, there was at least one church which held either a healing prayer service, an intercessors' group for the sick, prayer at Communion for individuals' needs, or prayer ministry after a service. But new ministers often had little experience of healing ministry, so they could echo Rev Trevor Dearing's remark of twenty years before: "At college they taught me how to bury the dead but not how to heal the sick!" Only some leaders had such training, and some of their healing services, though well-intentioned, varied in effectiveness.

Prayer for healing is needed for church members, but it's not the same as healing the sick everywhere, regardless of background. Peaceful prayer meetings can be beneficial, but powerful praise meetings are often more effective, for Spirit-led and Spirit-filled praise is one of the things that can release the power of the Holy Spirit (Ephesians 5:18-20).

By the year 2000 the emphasis was less on renewal itself, and—where desired—more about building on what had been discovered. This included new interest in the outreach commands.

My purpose in writing this is to help you catch this vision and encourage your leaders to do so as well. They may like to read about this, but, if they are not interested, perhaps the Holy Spirit will lead you to join or start a group that will take up the challenge!

CHAPTER 4

Preach the Gospel

Preaching the Gospel is always sharing the good news about Jesus Christ. Anything else is not the Gospel. Here I need to wax theological but to make it down-to-earth.

Significant Meanings

There have been many descriptions and presentations of the Gospel, both in the Bible and in the centuries since it was written. To help us all to understand how necessary this first and most important outreach command of Jesus really is, let's explore three great messages of the Gospel.

The First Gospel: Good News about God's Kingdom

When Jesus sent out His disciples on their own to preach the Gospel, they had several great advantages. They had probably been close to Jesus for two years or more, living, walking, talking, eating, and sleeping with Him. They had been trained for this mission. They had listened to His preaching and teaching on numerous occasions—no doubt noticing the authoritative but caring way He gave it—and had constantly observed His mighty works.

On the other hand, they were mainly uneducated and working-class men. They all knew Jesus as their Teacher and Master, as well as

Prophet and Healer, but they did not yet realise the full significance of why He had come to earth, nor taken it in that He would have to die and rise again. And even after His resurrection they still believed that He was going to rescue the Jews from Roman rule and set up His own kingdom here on earth.

However, Jesus gave them power and authority to fulfil their evangelistic mission, and what they *were* able to share about was what He'd taught about the Kingdom of God. Of course, they did not preach from pulpits but in homes and the open air, just as today ordinary Christians are called to preach the Gospel wherever they have the opportunity.

Jesus commanded them, "As you go, preach this message: the Kingdom of Heaven is near" (Matthew 10:7). You may know that the Kingdom of Heaven is exactly the same as the Kingdom of God. Because Matthew is writing to Jews, he avoids here the holy Name of God. But the disciples had listened—perhaps many times—to the same parables that Jesus preached about (earthly stories with Heavenly meanings), which often began with, "The Kingdom of Heaven is like ..."

Yet the Kingdom of Heaven is not Heaven—not the eternal realm where God sits enthroned, surrounded by angels, and where Christians go when they die or when Christ returns in body. The Kingdom of Heaven, or Kingdom of God, rather always refers to the reign or rule of God. This would be a familiar concept to the Jews, who, as the chosen nation, believed in God, but Jesus taught fresh things about it.

Whenever we pray, "Your Kingdom come", we are requesting God that more people will accept Him as their King. A king in those days exercised absolute power and authority, so to submit to God as King is to come under His power and authority. Jesus taught that He is the only Way to God and therefore the only Way into the Kingdom. To enter it, one must be born again and become like a little child. There are many blessings for those who enter the Kingdom but also many responsibilities, reminiscent of God's covenant with His chosen people. One day the Kingdom will be complete, and God will be seen and acknowledged as King by everyone everywhere. Until then we are to work for the spread of the Kingdom.

This was the message of those first disciples: "The Kingdom of God is near", for Jesus had come to make it possible for people to enter the

Kingdom. They were each encouraged to "repent, and believe the good news" (Mark 1:15). Today we may use some different phraseology, but our message is basically the same: the good news of Jesus Christ.

The Faith Gospel: Good News about Forgiveness

This is what we usually simply call **The Gospel**. It's the most important of all the many descriptions of good news about Jesus Christ because it affects our eternal destiny, and asserts how Christ alone was able to die on the cross to save us from eternal separation from God in hell. For this reason millions of Christians have gone to the ends of the earth—and still do — to ensure the Gospel is heard. But many people near at hand need to hear it too. The very best way I can explain the Gospel is with a series of relevant verses from the Bible:

> For all have sinned and fall short of the glory of God. (Romans 3:23)

> For the wages of sin is death, but the gift of God is eternal life through Jesus Christ our Lord. (Romans 6:23)

> But God demonstrates His love for us in this: While we were still sinners, Christ died for us. (Romans 5:8)

> For God so loved the world that He gave His one and only Son, that whoever believes in Him shall not perish but have eternal life. (John 3:16).

> Jesus answered, "I am the Way and the Truth and the Life. No one comes to the Father except through Me." (John 14:6)

> Salvation is found in no one else, for there is no other Name under heaven given to men by which we must be saved. (Acts 4:12)

To all who received Him, to those who believed in His Name, He gave the right to become children of God. (John 1:12)

Repent and be baptised, every one of you, in the Name of Jesus Christ for the forgiveness of your sins. And you will receive the Gift of the Holy Spirit. (Acts 2:38)

For it is by grace you have been saved, through faith—and this not of yourselves. It is the gift of God—not by works, so that no one can boast. (Ephesians 2:8–9)

Here I am! I stand at the door and knock. If anyone hears My voice and opens the door, I will come in and eat with him, and he with Me. (Revelation 3:20)

I am the Resurrection and the Life. He who believes in Me will live, though he dies: and whoever lives and believes in Me will never die. Do you believe this? (John 11:25–26)

By the amazing grace of God, and because of the atoning death of Christ, when someone repents of their sins and puts their trust in Christ to be their Saviour and Lord (whether or not they express it like that), God the Holy Spirit immediately goes to work in several ways:

- Their salvation is assured.
- All their sins are forgiven—and forgotten!
- The Spirit comes to live and stay within them forever.
- He begins to help them from the inside out.
- They each become an adopted child of God the Father.
- They receive eternal life.
- Their place is reserved in heaven.

The new Christian

- has been saved from the *penalty* of sin (justification),

- is constantly being saved from the *power* of sin (sanctification),
- and one day will be saved from the very *presence* of sin (glorification).

But salvation is a very big word. There is a lot more to it, as we shall see in the next section.

The Full Gospel: Good News about Wholeness

This description requires a much fuller explanation, partly because it *is* so full and partly because it is not so well-known outside of Pentecostal and Charismatic circles.

In Acts 5:20 an angel says to the apostles, "Tell the people the *full* message of this new life" (italics mine).

In Romans 15:18–19 St Paul recalls what he has been able to achieve for his Lord so far:

- He has led many *missions:* "from Jerusalem all the way round to Illyricum."
- He has preached many *messages:* "I have *fully* proclaimed the Gospel of Christ." (Italics mine).
- He has used three *methods:*
  (1) "By what I have *said*" — (God's words) — the verbal dimension (proclamation evangelism).
  (2) "By what I have *done*"— (God's ways) — the moral dimension (presentation evangelism).
  (3) "By the power of *signs and miracles*, through the power of the Spirit" — (God's works) — the supernatural dimension (power evangelism).

The apostle's words "fully proclaimed the Gospel of Christ" can equally be translated "the *full* Gospel of Christ". He certainly seems to be writing about more than the basic faith Gospel. As we have seen, the faith Gospel remains the only essential good news that someone needs to hear to be saved. The *full* Gospel is good news about Jesus Christ which may contain the basic Gospel but which also shares about other things that He has done, and that He is still doing, in the world of today. For we have so much good news to proclaim about His mighty transforming work by His Holy Spirit.

There are Full Gospel churches, such as at Seoul, South Korea—the largest church in the world—and Full Gospel organisations, such as the Full Gospel Businessmen's Fellowship International (FGBMFI) and its equivalent for ladies, Women Aglow.

The Pentecostals especially decided to proclaim four elements of the good news about Christ:

- Jesus as Saviour
- Jesus as Healer
- Jesus as Baptiser in the Holy Spirit
- Jesus as coming King.

Charismatics generally have the same wide vision, so that testimonies are not just about how someone once came to faith in Christ but how they've been changed, healed, baptised in the Spirit, set free from evil or harmful things, provided for, or protected by God.

- Sharing about Christ as Saviour mainly has to do with what He has done for us in the past.
- Speaking about Him as coming King has more to do with His promise to come in the future.
- Telling of Him as Healer or Baptiser may be about His work in our lives *now*.

Many people, recalling the fact that Christ is now at God's right hand in Heaven, may think of His main work as in the past. But as Man He could only be in one place at one time, while as Spirit He can be in every place and in all who invite Him. So He's working far more miracles now than then—sometimes separately, or through angels, but especially through believers.

That is important when exploring the outreach commands of Christ. We sing, "Only You can move the mountains," and that's true in the sense that only God or what is done in Jesus' Name can shift the biggest obstacles. But what the Lord actually said was, *"You* can say to this mountain, 'Go, throw yourself into the sea,' and it will be done" (Matthew 21:21). Again He was training His disciples not only to say what He was saying but to do what He was doing. He intended that they should!

Some preachers today give good expositions of the passages where Jesus or the early Church worked signs and wonders but seldom give instances of ones He is doing in our own day. You only have to search the internet, read particular books, or view Christian TV programmes to find examples. It may be that such preachers have become conditioned to the erroneous and discredited theory of cessationism—that no supernatural works—such as healings, miracles, or spiritual gifts—have occurred since the first few centuries after Christ (more about this in a later section of this investigation). Most preachers are likely to say they are not cessationists, but perhaps they act as if they *are.*

For Jesus has not even just risen from the dead. He's alive! He's here! He's the same—not only in who He is and in what He's like but in what He's doing. He used to heal people; He still does. He used to work miracles; He still does. And He can do these things through *you!*

Neither is He just setting unbelievers free from the penalty of sin. He's setting *Christians* free from harmful and evil things they have become bound to. He can do it through you too.

These are some aspects of the full Gospel. There are more.

Jesus came to earth to save sinners (1 Timothy 1:15)—to make them whole, not just to save their souls. The Christian can rejoice that "It is well with my soul", for Jesus died that our sins might be forgiven and He rose again "that we might go at last to Heaven."

However, when Jews were told that Jesus had come to save them, they were unlikely to be thinking in terms of body, mind, and soul (here meaning "spirit"). For, unlike the Greek philosophers, the Hebrews thought of themselves as whole persons. They would think that Christ had come to save *them*—their whole selves, not just their souls.

The old Greek word *sozo* can be translated either *saved, healed, delivered,* or *made whole,* according to the context. Jesus came to save people from *all* evils: "For this purpose Christ was revealed to destroy *all* the works of the evil one" (1 John 3:8)—not sin and death alone. He has triumphed over sin (as we have seen)—also over sickness (Isaiah 53:4–5 and Matthew 8:16–17), over Satan (Colossians 2:15), and even over death (1 Corinthians 15:55–57). All these are still with us, but Christ has won the victory over them and made it possible for us to have victory over them too, through faith in Him. So, "He is able to save *completely* those who come to God through Him" (Hebrews 7:25). We have been saved from so much, and we can be set free from so much as well!

He uses many kinds of people to bring healing: doctors, nurses, psychiatrists, therapists, counsellors, and self-help. He also brings it by His Spirit through Christians. There are many reasons why some people are not healed, and sometimes many conditions are required for complete healing. But, just as God wants all to be saved (2 Peter 3:9), His ideal will is for all to be made whole.

A key reference to the Full Gospel is Luke 4:18–19, which Jesus applies to Himself from Isaiah 61 and which we seek to follow as we preach His words and do His works today:

- The Spirit of the Lord is upon me, because He has anointed me to preach good news to the poor" (this is preaching the Gospel).
- He has sent me to proclaim freedom for the prisoners (deliverance),
- and recovery of sight for the blind (physical healing),
- to release the oppressed (inner healing),
- to proclaim the year of the Lord's favour ("Now is the day of salvation"— 2 Corinthians 6:2.)

Wholeness is not the same as perfection, which is a characteristic of God. It is more than becoming spiritually whole, although that is a perfectly legitimate and precious concept. It's been defined as complete wellbeing, or "the meeting of every genuine need as far as is possible in an imperfect world." The good news of the Full Gospel is that Jesus Christ is still able and willing to meet every need (Philippians 4:19). In fact, if you are a Christian He wants you to be holy, He wants you whole and He wants you healing!

Successful Methods

How can we preach the Gospel to unbelievers? Churches hold missions in different ways, but as far as individual believers are concerned there are four main contexts we can share it in:

Through Conversations

Particular situations where we may get the opportunity to talk to non-Christians about Jesus are when God leads us to, when it just arises, or when someone's interested.

Philip was the leader in the Samaritan revival, where signs and wonders were taking place (Acts 8:4–8), but God told him to leave there, and He sent him into the desert to talk to just one man (Acts 8:26–40). The Ethiopian "Chancellor of the Exchequer" was riding by when the Spirit said to Philip, "Go and glue yourself to that chariot!" Philip heard the man reading about God's Suffering Servant (Isaiah 53) and asked if he understood the passage. Philip was able to preach the Gospel to the man, who believed and was baptised.

If you get used to hearing the voice of God, like Philip He may sometimes guide you to be in the exact place and at the exact time where someone needs to hear you share about your faith. On some other occasions you may find yourself chatting to someone on a train or plane, for example, and something that is said opens up the way for you to share about your experience. And then there is the situation where a non-Christian has recently attended a service or read a Christian book or has seen a Christian video and perhaps wants to know more about them.

If you get filled with the Spirit you will have the boldness to share the Gospel (Acts 4:31). If you do not know what to say on a particular occasion, you can claim the wonderful promise that Jesus gave to persecuted disciples but which can apply to any situation: "Do not worry about what to say or how to say it, for it will not be you speaking, but the Spirit of your Father speaking through you" (Matthew 10:18–19). It's often a good idea to start with your own experience and to answer any questions if you can, but if you do not know the answer to a question, you might say, "I don't know," or "I'll find out for you."

Sometimes you may have opportunity to ask your own questions. Here are some examples:

- "Do you have a faith of any kind?"
- "Are you involved in any spiritual activities?"
- "What do you think about ... Christ?" (Matthew 22:42)
- "How would you like to live forever?"

If they are in particular need, you may add,

- "Have you thought of trying Christian healing?"

You may be just one link in God's plan for drawing someone to Himself. If you carry some Christian literature or a Christian DVD/CD, it may be the right time to offer this to the person.

Through Invitations

Several years before Philip met the Ethiopian official, a man called Philip had met Jesus for the first time at Cana. He told his friend Nathanael that he'd found the Messiah (John 1:45). But Nathanael was sceptical, so Philip urged, "Come and see." His friend did, and he soon found that Jesus knew all about him. Two years later, both Philip and Nathanael were among those Jesus sent out, and probably the same Philip was later in Samaria.

Like Philip, we may invite someone to where they may find Jesus or hear more about Him. Obviously it must be on a suitable occasion, perhaps at church or a Christian activity. Such an event must be where a newcomer's welcome and the Gospel's made relevant. The enquirer may only rarely have been to church, so it may be best if you go there together. (Note: because of a virus, church members might be meeting in their building, online, or in their homes.)

The worldwide popular Alpha Course is just one example of something that may interest someone concerned to discover more about the basics of Christianity. It may offer a meal, a message, a discussion, perhaps a video, and an opportunity to make some new friends over several weeks. Again, it can be found online during restrictions. You will need to be guided by the Holy Spirit. But inviting someone, perhaps who is already your friend, can be the start of their leading a changed life.

Through Proclamations

It looks as though the same Philip who *invited* his friend to meet Jesus and *conversed* with the Ethiopian about Him was probably the one who *proclaimed* Christ in Samaria. Some of you, like him, are called to be preachers in the public arena, perhaps in your local church. You probably had training to do this, so I'll just make one suggestion.

If you are already preaching the basic Gospel, that by Christ alone we can receive forgiveness of sins and eternal life, there is a need sometimes to give an opportunity for people to respond. This could be by leading them in a prayer of commitment, by inviting them to the front, or by indicating their desire to receive Christ as their Saviour in some other way.

Public preaching may be only one of the signposts on the way to someone's conversion, but sometimes it's the next step to challenging them gently after inviting them to church.

Through Demonstrations

Demonstrations of Love

In John 13:35 Jesus said, "By this all men will know that you are My disciples, if you love one another." He had previously added, "As I have loved you," for there would be nothing unusual in likeminded Jews bonding themselves together, but what made His commandment new was that it was with the sort of love that *He* had, an absolute *agape* love.

At Durham University I was president of the Christian Union. We were well known for our evangelistic zeal in seeking to be fishers of men, but sometimes we were more interested in "catching fish" than in caring for people. We are more likely to attract "fresh fish" if they see we care about them!

When I was a vicar at Huddersfield, a fellowship meeting held in our home was attended by people from a large estate who were not believers. But these were so overwhelmed by the love, warmth, and welcome given to them that they were soon surrendering their lives to Christ before they had heard very much about what it means to be a Christian.

Demonstrations of Power

Philip apparently used all the four methods that I have mentioned to win unbelievers, for his preaching was sealed by demonstrations of power: When the crowds heard Philip and saw the miraculous signs that he did, they all paid close attention to what he said. With shrieks evil spirits came out of many, and many paralytics and cripples were healed. (Acts 8:6–7)

This echoes others' experience, that accompanying signs confirmed the word (Mark 16:20).

When the apostle Paul shared the good news with intellectuals at Athens, it was through debate and discussion. This may be why only "a few men became followers of Paul and believed" (Acts 17:34). But, when Paul went to Corinth, he wrote afterwards about two things he should have done at Athens that he did do at Corinth:

- I resolved to know nothing while I was with you except Jesus Christ and Him crucified. (1 Corinthians 2:2)
- My message and preaching were not with wise and persuasive words, but with a demonstration of the Spirit's power. (verse 4)

For the Bible teaches that the Kingdom of God is one of *power,* not of words (or talk—1 Corinthians 4:20). St. Paul accompanied His proclamation with *power* evangelism—with healings and miracles— and these would attract others to Jesus.

Throughout our healing ministry, Chris and I have seen many people come to meetings in the first instance seeking healing of other kinds but then hearing the Gospel and trusting in Jesus. Healing ministry is still one of the best points of contact for evangelism. If only more leaders and preachers would follow Jesus' outreach commands and make healing and deliverance available, they would see more unbelievers come to Christ, just as these did in Bible times.

One Example

A man I shall call Malcolm was a lecturer at the British School of Osteopathy while Chris my wife was training there. One day she was talking to a patient in the clinic and remarked that we did healing. Malcolm overheard, and he soon got *conversing* over coffee with Chris. It transpired that he was seeking for reality in his life, and he had already sought for this in Buddhism and the New Age movement, but all without success. He read our story, *It Hurts to Heal,* with avid interest. Chris *invited* him to one of our Praise, Healing, and Renewal Services at Hildenborough, Kent. Not long afterwards, desperate and eager, he drove the eighty miles from Basingstoke. At the meeting he heard me *proclaiming* the good news of Christ. He also saw this *demonstrated,* as people there were healed and delivered. There were prophetic gifts manifested, and some people fell under the power of the Holy Spirit.

Malcolm received the laying-on-of-hands and was greatly blessed but was full of questions. So Chris and I *invited* Malcolm back to our home, which was then at nearby Tonbridge, where he relaxed while we *conversed* and prayed with him until 2 am. Suddenly, things made sense to him, and he said, "I know it up here now" (pointing to his head) "but I don't feel it down here" (pointing to his heart). A little later, however, after kneeling down and inviting Jesus into his heart, he said, "Now I feel it in here!" He had found the reality he had been looking for. He had come to know Jesus as his personal Saviour and Lord, and, with our encouragement, he shortly afterwards joined a church in Hampshire, which took him under its wing.

You have the command and you have the power. Whether you are like Daniel Chand, our dynamic UK healing evangelist, or if you are another trained evangelist, or simply an "ordinary Christian", you have the privilege and responsibility of preaching the Gospel.

CHAPTER 5

Heal the Sick

Alll genuine healing—as distinct from counterfeit healing—comes to us from God, whether it is aided by medicine, surgery, ministry, therapy, counselling, or self-help.

Healing Purposes

We have seen that healing is among the *signs* that can point people to Jesus and Who He is, as He once told John the Baptist (Matthew 11:4–5). It is also sometimes among the things which cause people to *wonder*, or be amazed, at what He has done.

But He did not heal just to *prove* that He was God but because He *is* God. It is in His nature to heal: "When Jesus landed and saw a large crowd, He had compassion on them and healed their sick" (Matthew 14:14). "Filled with compassion, Jesus reached out and touched the man. "I am willing," He said. "Be clean!" Immediately, the leprosy left him and he was cured" (Mark 1:41–42).

The chief way Jesus showed that He cared about the needs of people was by healing their sick.

If we are to do the works of Jesus, we not only need to obey His commands but to have His love, which the Holy Spirit can give us.

Healing Sources

The New Testament tells us about four kinds of people who can bring about or aid genuine healing: physicians (Mark 2:17), church leaders (James 5:14), Christian people with gifts or ministries of healing (1 Corinthians 12:9 and 28), and "ordinary" believers (Mark 16:17–18).

Christian healing ministry includes the general healing ministry of the Church in churches, homes, and hospitals, particular campaigns by healing evangelists and others with gifts and ministries of healing, and the Spirit-led or spontaneous ministry that any Christians can do.

Healing Foundations

There are two solid foundations of Christian healing. If anyone has any doubts about either of these, this may cause them not to be so effective when ministering to the sick and needy.

- God's ability and willingness to heal (Matthew 14:14; Mark 1:41–42; Luke 4:18–19).
- The Church's commission to heal (Mark 6:7–13; Mark 16:14–20; Luke 10:1–12).

Healing Areas

When Jesus told His disciples and others to heal the sick, He was almost certainly thinking especially of the physically sick. Many of these would be in the streets and lanes, where He cured them. But we have already seen that He also wants people to be made completely whole. So we also read of Him healing the sick in mind, fractured relationships among His disciples, and disturbing circumstances.

There are six main areas of need that are included in the Christian ministry of wholeness:

Relationship with God (salvation)

(Acts 2:21; Acts 16:30–31; 2 Corinthians 5:20)

Jesus made it clear that this is the most important kind of healing: "It is better for you to lose one part of your body than for your whole body to go into hell" (Matthew 4:30). So we must not dodge the sin problem. When someone comes to us in great pain, our first concern will be to ensure that the pain is removed or eased. But that individual may have to be told at some point about their need of reconciliation with God through Christ. We have already seen that this is one of our aims when we have opportunity to preach the Gospel.

Physical Healing

(Matthew 10:1; Mark 16:17–18; James 5:14–16)

It is important to notice that there is a big distinction in the New Testament between physical sickness and other types of suffering. For example, in Matthew 20 Christ expects His disciples to suffer persecution, but he does not tell the two blind men to put up with their physical suffering. He asks them, "What do you want Me to do?" and He gives them their sight. Jesus regards sickness as an evil to be overcome.

Since, as we have seen, the Lord normally wants to make people whole in some way (not necessarily the way we expect), it is unwise to pray "If it is Your will" for physical healing. We can unintentionally be adding a measure of doubt to our prayers, and the sick person hearing our prayer is hardly likely to be encouraged! Jesus wanted to heal all who came to Him for healing, and He's the same Jesus.

It is unwise too to promise complete healing, unless this is also confirmed by someone else. However, it's important to pray specifically, positively and expectantly, while without giving false hopes. In addition to praying for restoration, we may ask for prevention or improvement.

Inner Healing (of mind, will, and emotions)

(Psalm 147:3; Luke 4:18–19; Philippians 4:6–7)

This is often the focus of prayer counselling as well as prayer ministry. In prayer counselling the trained Christians will listen at length to the person's needs, then lay on hands and pray, while listening to the Lord in case He has things to show them that will help towards healing.

The sufferer is often encouraged to relive the root cause of his or her concerns, such as an accident, illness, bereavement, or difficult relationship. This is what Christ did to Peter, who had disowned Him in front of a charcoal fire (John 18:18). Jesus put him in front of another charcoal fire, challenged him, forgave him, and gave him another chance (John 21:15).

A common need in inner healing is healing of hurts and painful memories. The person is encouraged to trust Jesus—who is the same yesterday, today, and forever—to go back into their yesterdays (Hebrews 13:8). By faith-imagination Jesus is placed in the centre of the original painful situation, and we trust Him to take away the hurt. After this ministry the person may still remember the circumstances but without pain.

Deliverance

(Matthew 18:18; Luke 4:18–19; Ephesians 6:10–18)

We shall explore this one in detail in chapter 7 of this investigation: "Drive Out Demons." Note that Jesus always included it in His commands when sending people to preach and heal.

Restoring of Relationships

(Genesis 45:1–15; Ephesians 4:32; Philippians 4:2–3)

Chris and I once led a young married couple to put their trust in Christ for their salvation. Then it transpired that the wife had committed adultery, and her husband refused to forgive her. But we reminded him that when he was a lost sinner Jesus had died for him that he might be forgiven. Eventually the husband forgave her aloud, and the moment that he did he went down on the floor in the power of the Holy Spirit.

Healing of Circumstances

(Daniel 6:19–23; Acts 16:25–26; Acts 27:22–26)

The Bible references I have given here illustrate the different ways God deals with difficult circumstances, especially when we pray about them.

Sometimes He *changes* them, as when Paul and Silas were in the dungeon at Philippi praising the Lord and the earthquake of AD 44 happened just at that moment. As a result, the jailor and his household came to trust in Christ. In a similar way some people are instantly healed when they have received the touch of Jesus.

Sometimes God *checks* the circumstances, as when He delivered Daniel from being devoured in the den of lions, but the prophet still had to wait until the morning before being released. Similarly, some sick people find their condition stabilises before they get completely better.

And sometimes the Lord *cheers* the circumstances, as when He showed Paul that he and his companions would be shipwrecked at Malta but that they would all escape safely to land. So too we sometimes have to go through really difficult situations, but the Lord is with us as we do, and we have His promise that He will never leave us or forsake us (Hebrews 13:5).

Healing Concerns

Church leaders especially sometimes have concerns about launching healing ministry in their churches: "I have little experience of this ministry. There is no one in my congregation who has had a gift of healing. Will I be able to keep things under control? What will the other church leaders think? Suppose nothing obvious happens, or no one gets healed? Where will it all lead? Suppose it's taken to extremes?" Church members also sometimes hold back from praying for complete healing for fear that nothing will happen and they will be embarrassed.

All these fears are understandable and genuine. But none of these things must prevent us if we decide that the Lord wants us to go ahead. He will honour us if we are faithful to His command. Whatever the outcome, the results department is with Him. Be prepared to be a fool for Christ's sake (1 Corinthians 3:18)! Yes, you will make mistakes. Yes, not everyone will be healed. Yes, you may face some opposition. But, if you are following the Holy Spirit's leading, you are likely to be encouraged.

Some churches need scriptural teaching about healing and wholeness before offering regular healing ministry. Sometimes a guest preacher with healing experience can help here. Pray that God will raise up those who will minister in a healing team. How it is done in your own churches may differ from others, so it's important to find the best way for *your* church. One church I knew of persevered for ten months before they saw an obvious healing.

You may find some things in this investigation will help and encourage you to step out in faith. And that is usually the best way round. Do not wait until you have all the answers (you never will!) Our experience is that, when we step out in faith and pray for healing, the Lord provides all that is needed: the love, the guidance, the words, the gifts, and the healing, will all be there.

Healing Strategy

A church leader may have various reasons for starting healing ministry. It may be requested by the congregation, or a Christian doctor, or grow out of a prayer group. The main thing is that the leader has some vision or enthusiasm for this and believes God desires it.

In this ministry some ministers major on anointing with oil, some on Communion, some on words of knowledge. We allow for this while majoring ourselves on the laying-on-of-hands.

We have encouraged the regular laying-on-of-hands in a church, such as once a month in a service, so people know when to expect it. We have also encouraged church groups always to have available someone capable to minister to anyone who is sick or in great pain.

At the Sunday service the laying-on-of-hands may be offered after the sermon, during the prayers, with the Communion, at the close of the service, or separately after the service. There are several advantages when the healing ministry can take place within a service. It can be seen as a ministry of the whole body of Christ in that place, it may attract people who would not otherwise come to church, and can be a demonstration of the Holy Spirit.

A good idea in this context is for each person coming forward for prayer to be asked to mention only one need. And the congregation can sing while the ministry is proceeding. Alternatively, when the ministry is in a small gathering, each person to be prayed for can stand in the centre of a circle of people. In training sessions the audience may be split into groups in different parts of the building. If words of knowledge are given, the particular people they may refer to may be invited to the front of the building for specific ministry. United healing prayer services have often been held on weeknights, training sessions at weekends.

While ministering, the team may sense that some people require further ministry or prayer counselling. Some may need following up in their homes, or in hospital. Others may need specialist help, and be referred to doctors or reputable therapists. The team may meet regularly to pray and discuss these issues and to seek the guidance of the Holy Spirit. We also encourage Christians to minister in their daily lives when opportunities arise.

Healing Methods

Some of these, when under virus restrictions, may only be possible in certain circumstances.

Do not get stuck at James 5! There, in verses 13–20, we have several procedures laid out for us as to what to do about praying for the sick in our own church. While I rejoice at seeing any healing ministry, I am surprised that so many church leaders only follow what James was recommending for the housebound sick of his own church, one of the earliest Christian ones.

God is a God of variety (1 Corinthians 12:4–6). And did you know that in the Gospels Jesus used more than thirty different means of bringing healing? The following list is not exclusive:

The Healing Prayer Service

(Acts 14:8–10; 1 Corinthians 14:26–32; James 5:13–20)

We have already seen some of the advantages and ingredients of this. It should include if possible worship and the word. There are so many false ideas and misunderstandings about sickness and healing, and the preaching here can help people see Jesus as the Great Healer.

Holy Communion

(Luke 22:14–20; John 6:51–57; 1 Corinthians 11:25–30)

This is a healing sacrament but not a magical one. Usually some sort of response is required from the worshipper. Where people are used to going forward to receive the Communion, it may be best for participants to do this first and then remain where they are for specific prayer. Where people are used to remaining in their seats for the Communion, it may be best to make the healing ministry a separate activity. As with everything else, the leaders should seek the Lord to see how He wants it done in their context. Either way there can be great blessing!

Laying-On-Of-Hands

(Mark 7:33–35; Mark 16:17–18; Luke 4:40)

In the Scriptures laying-on-of-hands is used in connection with penitence (Leviticus 16:21), assurance (Revelation 1:17), receiving the Holy Spirit (Acts 8:17), commissioning and ordaining (Acts 13:3), and specific blessing (Mark 10:16), as well as healing (Mark 16:18). It is not a mechanical process but neither is it a dead symbol. Healers who are not Christians have found it can help to bring effective healing through a release of energy. How much more can it be effective if given in the Name of Jesus and in the power of the Holy Spirit! We can offer it as the touch of Jesus, and say that those who receive it will be blessed in some way. The gentle touch may be on someone's head, shoulder, the affected part of their body (such as Jesus did in John 9:6), an arm wrapped around them, or simply holding their hand. In TV and virtual services, those watching lay hands on themselves while prayer is offered.

Soaking Prayer

(Mark 5:27–30; Mark 8:22–26; John 9:6–7)

Many people need a second touch, like the blind man Jesus healed who first saw people like trees walking (Mark 8:22–26). Many are not completely healed immediately, like the ten lepers who found that "as they went, they were cleansed" (Luke 17:14). And a number need a series of regular sessions of healing. When a person shows signs of improvement after one or two sessions of laying-on-of-hands, we have often found that it is beneficial to offer soaking prayer—usually a course of treatment in relaxed surroundings. We've kept our hands on the sufferer's body for long periods of time—say twenty to thirty minutes—while praying aloud, worshipping in song, or talking informally while the Spirit's power flows through.

Anointing with Oil

(Mark 6:13; Luke 10:34; James 5:14)

This was used at the commissioning of priests and kings. It became a symbol of God the Holy Spirit's anointing. It was part of first aid in Bible times, when the first Christians also used it effectively in healing ministry. Nowadays, in some denominations, it is utilised only by the leaders, who may make the sign of the cross on the person's forehead. We especially use it on sick believers when they request it. It is another means of ministering the touch of Jesus.

A famous entertainer's son fell off a cliff and was badly injured. The family were Christians, and after their pastor had anointed him with oil he quickly recovered and was fully restored.

The Spoken Word

(2 Kings 20:4–6; Matthew 8:13; James 5:15–18)

A centurion once recognised that, if Jesus spoke a word, his servant would be healed. We shall look at this more in chapter 7, on casting out demons, but the right word spoken in Jesus' name—even if it is not a prophecy or a word of wisdom—can be another means by which needy people find improvement. Trust the Lord and He will show you what to say.

Command Prayers

(Matthew 8:3; Luke 4:39; Acts 16:16–18)

We have no record of Jesus ever using request prayers for the sick. These are acceptable for us to use today, for He said, "You may ask Me for *anything* in My Name and I will do it" (John 14:14). And James wrote, "Pray for each other that you may be healed" (James 5:16).

But in the New Testament there is only one request prayer for healing: "Stretch out Your hand to heal" (Acts 4:30), and that is a general prayer such as we might use in a liturgy. All of the others are *command* prayers of authority used with individuals—not ones like "Lord, heal our friend's lameness" but "Friend, in the Name of Jesus rise up and walk!" So if we only pray request prayers we are again only using some of the equipment that God has provided for us. Of course I should only tell a lame person to rise and walk if the Holy Spirit guides me to or if I manifest a *Gift* of faith (1 Corinthians 12:9), which is different from my everyday faith. But it only requires a little faith to pray command prayers like "Be healed" or "Find healing", as long as the sufferer understands that it is up to God as to how and when it will happen. I believe that the more we use His commands the more we are likely to see more healings.

The Word of Knowledge

(1 Kings 14:4–6; John 1:51; John 4:18)

This is the most recorded supernatural gift in the Bible. It can be so valuable in healing, as the Lord shows a Christian something they could not attain by memory, reason, or investigation—perhaps an underlying need, the root cause of a problem, or that Jesus is healing the person.

Once I was leading a healing service when I suddenly knew that God was healing someone's eyes. I announced this to the congregation, and a lady who was present claimed it for herself. Afterwards we discovered that she had been cured there of glaucoma and ingrown eyelids.

Confessing Faults

(Acts 19:18–20; James 5:15–16; 1 John 1:7–9)

This too can lead to physical healing. It is especially valuable when Christians share about their own sins and mistakes before taking Communion, and it can be a liberating experience. However, it requires able leadership, as there is no point in holding long, morbid, and inward-looking sessions. Also, those present must keep confidences and hand things over to the Lord. James is aware that sometimes diseases are the result of sin, and he reminds us that, when the sufferer receives healing, God will forgive him for the sin at the same time.

Forgiving Others

(Luke 6:37; Ephesians 4:32; Colossians 3:13)

If we keep resenting those who have wronged us, this may rob us of peace. We may require God's help to enable us to forgive them. When we do, this can restore peace and healing to us.

Richard was a man suffering from a stomach disorder. He received laying-on-of-hands and felt much better. But when his problem returned he had more ministry. Again he felt better but was soon worse again. A third time he went for healing, and this time he confessed that he bitterly resented his parents and the way they had treated him. He was encouraged to forgive them aloud, and received healing for his hurts. This time after the ministry he not only felt much better, but the healing of his stomach disorder proved to be complete and permanent.

Deliverance

(Matthew 18:18; Luke 4:18–19; Ephesians 6:10–18)

We'll consider this in detail when we come to chapter 7 of our exploration: "Drive Out Demons."

Positive Thinking

(Matthew 21:18–22; Philippians 4:13; James 5:15)

This is not "mind over matter". Research has found that negative thoughts and words can cause a person's cells to vibrate and so contribute to disease. And we have found that negative thoughts, as well as negative words, can restrict healing. When ministering, we have sought to picture the sufferer in a healthy condition, such as the crippled walking, the blind seeing, and the depressed laughing.

Prayer Counselling

(Luke 4:18–19; John 21:15–17; Acts 8:26–40)

As we saw under *Inner Healing,* this prolonged ministry does not involve giving advice but listening, prayer ministry and spiritual gifts. It is normally carried out by trained Christians helping other believers with deep needs, as God guides. Each one may need several sessions.

Encouragement to Respond

(John 2:5; Acts 3:7; Acts 14:9–10)

Some people who come for prayer need to be encouraged to relax. They might also be told what they might do towards receiving their healing, as there is often something required.

A woman was healed of heart trouble at an Anglican healing prayer service. Later a lump came up in her body, and when Rodney the vicar asked her what she needed prayer for, she said in a quiet voice, "Strength to cope with this."

Rodney then asked, "Are you sure that's *all* that you want me to pray for?"

"Well," she replied, "I really want to be completely better, of course."

Leading a Balanced Life

(Proverbs 3:7–8; Mark 2:17; James 1:5)

The woman who wants to lose weight must naturally eat appropriate foods. The man who is suffering from stress may have to cut down his commitments. The needy can become more whole as they look to Jesus but are also prepared to take charge of their own health care.

Ensuring a Healing Atmosphere

(Matthew 13:58; Luke 5:17; Acts 2:42–47)

A service where there is a lot of unbelief, resentment or opposition can obviously restrict rather than aid the flow of healing. But leaders can otherwise help to ensure an appropriate atmosphere. One of faith, love, and support can aid healing. So too can particular things which help to release the power of the Holy Spirit. These include especially Spirit-led and Spirit-filled praise and worship, authoritative preaching of the Word, united expectant prayer, laying-on-of-hands, and supernatural gifts of the Holy Spirit, such as prophecy, words of knowledge, tongues and interpretation, and other manifestations.

Occasionally people have been healed just by being in a healing atmosphere. This happened often at Kathryn Kuhlman's meetings and has occurred at *Christ for All Nations* crusades.

Healing Principles

We recommend that those ministering healing follow these principles. The initial letters spell *PERSON*. Each sick or needy individual is not just a case but a person loved through and through by Jesus. The "treatment" can be holistic and gentle but positive and powerful.

Point them to Jesus

He is the Great Physician, it's His touch we minister, our faith is in Him and the results department is with Him. We encourage the sufferer to keep his or her eyes upon Jesus throughout the prayer ministry and to give Him the glory.

Every case is different

God may heal the same person or condition in a different way from last time. Those ministering are encouraged to follow the Spirit's guidance on each occasion: listening, asking questions, sharing gifts, and using their experience.

Root cause (find it)

This is not always essential, but sometimes the person is not entirely healed until it is discovered. When there's a multiplicity of needs it's usual to pray first about the spiritual ones, then underlying ones, then have prayer for physical healing.

Step out in Faith

Once we know that it is time to minister, we can offer Jesus' touch (the laying-on-of-hands or anointing). Then, once we have begun to pray, the right words, the Lord's love, the healing power, and any other gifts, should begin to flow.

One step at a time

Unless we know that the complete answer to our prayers will come at once, we should pray within our faith, one step at a time. As our confidence grows we may pray for bigger things, until we discover that our goal has been achieved.

No condemnation

Even if individuals confess a terrible sin, we should not condemn them. We do not condone the sin, but, when there is an appropriate moment, we should lovingly encourage the person to repent of the sin and respond accordingly.

Healing Keys

Healing may be delayed or missed completely if those concerned do not discover and use the appropriate tools that God has provided. There are six major keys to Christian healing. When someone has seen little or no progress, even after plenty of medicine and ministry, one or more of the keys required may be lacking. That may be why a sick person has not yet been completely cured. Look for the appropriate keys and apply them, and my experience is that something good will always happen, because one of these keys frequently unlocks a door to the next stage.

Faith

(Mark 6:5; John 14:12; James 5:15)

It's not wise to suggest someone is not healed because of their lack of faith. But if a person fails to exercise faith this can obstruct healing, as Jesus once found at Nazareth (Mark 6:5). We encourage people to put their faith in the Lord, and someone *must* put their faith in Christ for their own salvation. But for physical healing other Christians may have faith for them.

Sometimes people are not healed because Christians are not praying for them within their faith. Rather than claiming the promise of James 5:15, they pray the prayer of hope, thinking, "If God wants to heal this person, He will." The Lord may answer that prayer, but He doesn't promise to. He *does* promise to answer the prayer of faith, of expectancy. So pray only for what you can believe for. But also aim for your faith to grow, and to expect more from God. If at the moment someone can believe for more than you can, let that person take the lead in the prayer ministry, but back them up by praying for them until the Lord's answer is clear.

Guidance

(John 14:26; James 1:5; Revelation 3:22)

Some people remain unhealed because those ministering are not following God's leading. Walking in the Holy Spirit includes listening to His voice and looking for His guidance in different places. And we've already seen that He may want to guide us one step at a time. It does not usually mean that He wishes to heal someone at a particular time in the future, though He may. Usually He wants them healed as soon as possible, just as a parent desires their child healed as soon as possible. But the surgeon must have all of the correct facilities before he will perform an operation, and God desires us to be in the right place at the right time and following His instructions. He may give these to us in total or separately.

Love

(John 13:34; 1 Corinthians 13; 2 Corinthians 5:14)

Doctors have shown that physical conditions may be the result of negative attitudes. For example, arthritis usually means there is wear and tear on the body, but it may be linked with resentment. This does not mean that everyone with arthritis is full of bitterness, but, if the arthritic person forgives someone who's hurt them, that may help speed restoration.

Once at a healing prayer service there was a hostile atmosphere until the children were ministered to. A wave of compassion swept over the congregation as children were blessed by Doctor Jesus.

Gifts of the Holy Spirit

(Matthew 10:8; Mark 16:17–20; 1 Corinthians 12:1–11 and 28)

As we have seen, some believers hold back from sharing these—such as prophecy or words of knowledge—because of fear they will get something wrong, or that the sick person will gain false hopes. But, when Christians are bold to say what God is showing them, this can again pinpoint a need or reveal what Jesus is doing. We've also seen that, once we step out in faith, everything needed will flow to us and through us. If you do make a mistake, confess it and learn from it. Remember that the big and specific promises should be confirmed by others.

A Release of Power

(Mark 5:30; Luke 5:17; Acts 3:12 and 16)

This is why most Christians who witness people frequently healed through their ministry have consciously been filled with the Holy Spirit. And the two chief ways in which we can release the power are by opening our mouths (e.g. in worship) and our hands (e.g. in the laying-on-of-hands).

A Willingness to Change

(2 Kings 5:11–14; Mark 10:50–52; John 5:6)

Naaman the leper is a good example of this. At first he was unwilling to consult a prophet, preferring to go to a king. Next he did not want to listen to a messenger, instead of Elisha himself. Then he hated the idea of bathing in the foreign muddy River Jordan! But, once he followed the way God wanted to heal him, his flesh became like that of a young boy.

Healing Progress

Chris and I have witnessed a number of people instantly healed, especially of blindness, deafness, paralysis, trapped nerves, hernias, muscular pain, and back trouble. But most of our healings have been gradual. So it's important to remember to "keep on knocking until the door is opened" (Matthew 7:8). Many Christians give up too soon! If a healing evangelist or teacher comes to town, the churches need to follow up the ministry by praying further with those who need healing and request it. Or, if there is a healing prayer service in a church, the prayer ministry team or others should take opportunities to pray with those concerned until they are satisfied. The results department is God's, but we are the ones He works through.

One Example

Someone who was healed over a period is Pam. She was a Christian who worshipped at Holy Trinity Church, Brompton, and was so keen on winning others to Christ that she would leave tracts and other Christian literature in waiting rooms and telephone boxes in parts of London. Pam had tried various sources to find healing for her eye trouble. Then a lady who attended our Praise, Healing and Renewal meetings kept enthusing to Pam about our healing ministry. Pam was somewhat suspicious of what we might be like! But eventually she invited us to her home. At that time Chris and I used to travel to minister healing to people in their homes within a 25-mile radius of where we then lived. Pam lived mainly in Kensington, London, but we travelled to minister to her in her holiday home at Rustington, on the West Sussex coast.

By then her disease of the eyelids had been diagnosed at Moorfields Hospital as medically incurable, and she was told it would lead to blindness, so she was desperate to find a cure.

After we had laid hands on Pam and prayed with her once a month for four months, she was gradually able to come off every one of the antibiotics and steroids she had been taking to keep clear of infection and to ease the constant irritation. But her underlying condition remained.

It then stabilised. Each time we ministered there was some improvement, but, before we were due to visit Pam again, she would experience a slight deterioration. Once or twice she waited longer than usual before calling us, and at such times her condition appeared to worsen. However, when we both laid hands on her the Lord brought her back to the point of stability that she had enjoyed before. It was one of those cases where we had to keep on knocking.

Eventually we traced the root cause of Pam's problem to a fall many years previously when she had dislocated her neck. When we prayed about this, she soon experienced complete healing of her eyes. For well over thirty years she loved to tell everyone about the healing that Jesus had given her. Not long ago, Pam joyfully celebrated her hundredth birthday at her care home at Henley-on-Thames. And a few months afterwards she went to Heaven.

Healing Importance

It might be easy to think of the healing ministry as an optional extra in your local church, but if we view needy people with the caring eyes of Jesus we should see it as a priority. Everyone knows someone who is ill or in great need. Interceding for them is a great thing to do. We can also pray for them by proxy, by receiving the laying-on-of-hands and having ministry for them. But ideally it's best for the person to be physically present to receive the powerful touch of Jesus.

CHAPTER 6

Cleanse the Lepers

In the twentieth century people used to refuse to touch others who had HIV or AIDS for fear of catching it, but Princess Diana had no hesitation about touching them. Similarly in the first century people refused to touch lepers, but Jesus not only touched them but healed them too.

Leprosy then

Lepers, who might have sores all over their bodies, were forced to live apart from normal society in colonies. In Israel they were regarded as ritually unclean as well as contagious. But some of them must have heard that Jesus cured sick people. So ten lepers, for instance, once "stood at a distance and called out in a loud voice, 'Jesus, Master, have pity on us!'" (Luke 17:12–13). On that occasion He just said, "Go, show yourselves to the priests."

Today, if someone believes they have been cured of a serious illness through prayer ministry, we encourage them to ask their doctor to confirm the cure before they share about it. But in olden days that was the task of the local priests. "And as they went they were cleansed." That meant also the healing of relationships, as lepers who had been segregated were reunited with relatives. They could live normally with their families, friends, and neighbours.

There are no recorded accounts in the Bible of Jesus' disciples healing people of leprosy. But He would not have told them to do this if He was not confident that they could. Probably such incidents would be among the many signs and wonders they performed. What we can be sure of is that the seriousness of an illness did not deter them from ministry.

Leprosy Later

Following the early centuries of the Christian era, descriptions of the Church's work among lepers is sketchy. It's not until the nineteenth century that we discover much more. Since then good work has been done by the Leprosy Mission and others in treating and caring for lepers and attending to their spiritual needs. Also, dedicated people have devoted their lives to the lepers' cause, such as Father Damien, to the extent that he eventually became one of them.

Occasionally there were instances of miraculous healings, and once again the Pentecostals were among the first to achieve these. During the early years of the twentieth century there were thousands of lepers in South Africa. Many had their fingers off at the first joint, some at the second joint, with their thumbs off or nose off, their teeth gone, their toes off, or their bodies scaling off. At Holy Communion on Christmas Eve 1912 those who had no fingers on their hands had to take the cup between their wrists. But many were cured through the ministry of a poor native South African, who not long before had worn only a goatskin apron. He had been converted through Pentecostals and in turn many through him were healed.

It's significant that widespread spiritual revival has taken place more often in societies and cultures that are more primitive, and part of the developing world, than in the sophisticated countries of the West, where often Christians cannot even believe that miracles are possible today. The knowledge and education of people like that native South African may not be great, but they sometimes have a simple faith which says, "Jesus used to perform miracles, He's the same today, so I trust Him to do what no one else is able to do!"

Leprosy Now

During the long Charismatic Renewal we should not be surprised that miraculous cures from leprosy were reported, and occasionally they still are, though these seldom find a place in the secular media, and only occasionally in the Christian press. Incidents are few and far between. This is partly, of course—as we have seen—because leprosy is not such a big issue in our own country today. But there are still some believers that the Lord is calling to work in this area.

One Example

During 1985 two Filipino nurses were working in a Gulf state at an Arab hospital. With childlike simplicity they believed that Jesus healed lepers. No one had suggested that such things could not happen today. Not only were lepers healed through these nurses but the parts which had been missing and had dropped off their bodies reappeared, whole. The church there, with twenty members, grew as a result to two thousand in two years.

Leprosy Principle

Most of us will probably not have to deal with leprosy. But the principle is just the same in connection with other diseases and conditions which are the equivalents of leprosy today. Though tremendous advances have been made through medical science, especially in the realm of genetics, there are people with serious illnesses that doctors can do no more for. Doctor Jesus can! A healing evangelist has held an annual service for "incurables", often with great results. Christ can also help the outcasts of society. And He can do it through us!

CHAPTER 7

Drive Out Demons

Some things in the Bible described as demonic we may class today as mental illness. But make no mistake: demons are very real, Jesus dealt with them, and so too must the Church. Just as the New Testament distinguishes between sicknesses and other types of suffering, it distinguishes clearly between driving out evil spirits and healing sickness (Matthew 10:1).

How It Arises

Demons only tend to manifest themselves among Christians when the Holy Spirit's power is released, and even when Jesus met them His Presence was not enough to cast them out. They had to be commanded to leave, which is something else He has authorised believers to do.

In the middle of the twentieth century there was a surge of interest in the occult. This area, more than any other, attracted evil spirits to invade some people's lives. For it involved them in the supernatural realm, from which the devil directs the activities of his agents. But God is good! When the Charismatic Renewal burst upon the Church scene there were many Christians who became equipped to cast out demons, and what a difference it made to the people concerned!

However, untrained, fearful, and inexperienced Christians should never take the lead in actual exorcism ministry—rather they can observe, support, and pray for those who have experience. This is not because Satan has anywhere near the power of God, for "the One that is in you is greater than the one that is in the world" (1 John 4:4)—but because there are some necessary procedures to follow to ensure both the success of the ministry and the safety of all concerned.

In this chapter we shall look not only at exorcism but the wider deliverance ministry. This is based on the victory that Christ has won for us over sin, sickness, Satan, and death. Believers have been given His authority to triumph over all these things in His powerful Name. And, though as individuals we are sometimes defeated, as His Church we are on the victory side.

Christians sometimes think of the Church as a bit like a cruise ship, with all comforts and pleasures provided. But John Wimber pointed out that it's more like a battleship, for Jesus expects us not only to refuse to yield to temptation but sometimes to attack the enemy. That is what deliverance ministry—setting people free from things—is all about. All Christian deliverance is done in the powerful Name of Jesus. This is not a superstitious or magical formula but our badge of authority from our Captain. So it means that when we use His Name and put our trust in Him to deliver people, we expect powerful things to happen.

Let's look now, then, at the four main types of deliverance:

Standing Firm

"Resist the devil, and he will flee from you" (James 4:7). This is the simplest form of deliverance, for any believer on their own. When evil forces come against you, in whatever shape or form, you can come against them with the authority of Christ, by speaking out loud the powerful Name of Jesus.

Setting Free

Jesus also gave believers the authority to release people from harmful things. He promised, "Whatever you loose on earth will be loosed in Heaven" (Matthew 18:18). This is the most common form of deliverance, and something else any Christian can do led by the Holy

Spirit. However, it's usually best for inexperienced people to let the experienced ones take the lead.

When a problem is small it may be overcome by our own prayers, like a piece of string being cut. But when a problem is like a big chain around us we need others to unlock the chains or use the sword of the Spirit, and to say things like "We set you free in Jesus' Name."

Ancestral Ties

Both sins and sicknesses may "run in the family" (Exodus 20:5), so, while we thank God for everything good that people have inherited, we ask the Lord for them each to be set free from their parents and ancestors, so that harmful things are cut off at the root. Obviously they must play their part in this. It's no good someone saying, "My father was lazy so I always will be!"

Authority Figures

Some believers are psychologically bound in a harmful way to people in authority, such as parents, teachers, doctors, police or pastors. When we cut them free this may in some cases have to be reinforced several times, until all the fear or bondage has gone, at least from the conscious mind.

Addictions and Habits

If someone becomes addicted to something that is not good for them—drugs, violence, sex, gambling or whatever—they may find help from others but it may only be as they receive deliverance ministry in Jesus' Name that they are sure of breaking the chains completely.

Attitudes and Inabilities

We can deliver someone from a negative attitude and minister the opposite to this: love for fear, forgiveness for resentment, peace for anxiety, assurance for guilt, healing of memories for hurt. In each case the person must be willing to be changed by God's transforming power.

We can also minister new abilities, things that do not come naturally or easily to someone. For example, we can pray that a person who is indecisive can become decisive, or that someone who is inflexible can become flexible.

Sending Off

Sending evil spirits from places they are haunting or oppressing is something else in which experienced people should take the lead. The results are often nothing short of miraculous. For example, when we have cleansed a "haunted house" in every part, the residents who before would not dream of living in them have found such a different and happy atmosphere.

Casting Out (Exorcism)

Believers who cast out demons find it a satisfying but costly experience. Sometimes this can mean spending several days in prayer and fasting, but it is well worth it. We may need to know in which areas Satan has a hold upon someone and consequently how to minister. There is no point in looking for evil spirits, and no need to fear them if we walk with the Lord. However, should we discern their presence, we have authority to deal with them.

Although new believers may have renounced evil and occult involvement, Satan may still have a hold on them in a related area that they've forgotten, so deliverance may be necessary.

Casting out demons involves directly challenging them. While the touch is frequently used for healing, we use the word for deliverance. So Jesus "drove out the spirits with a word" (Matthew 8:16). A command prayer of authority is essential to challenge each to leave. Evil spirits must be told to go, even if they are not inhabiting a person's body. They will depart eventually if commanded to in Jesus' Name and if those people they have gained a hold on have renounced and forsaken them. We tell them to go where Jesus sends them. Since a person has wittingly or unwittingly invited a spirit in by an act of his or her will, it may only go if renounced along with the sins that originally attracted it to gain hold. But if you are not sure and you seek the Lord, He will show you when a person is completely free.

Afterwards we are responsible too for ensuring the released captive is given care, prayer and fellowship, and that they keep close to God and away from evil things.

Discerning and Rebuking

I believe every church needs at least one person who has manifested the gift of discerning of spirits. It enables them to know whether someone is speaking or acting motivated by the Holy Spirit, their human spirit, or an evil spirit. This is a "lonely gift", since what the discerner sees may not be recognised by others. But these things may also become clear in other ways, especially when power is released through Spirit-led and Spirit-filled worship and other spiritual gifts. For it's usually essential to know what we are dealing with, so that we are not deceived by Satan's agents. We can then minister deliverance confidently.

The Lord Jesus Christ rebuked evil and harmful things, such as a demon (Matthew 17:18), a fever (Luke 4:39), and the storm on the Sea of Galilee (Mark 4:39). We can rebuke harmful things too. He has also given us authority to bind them:

- "Whatever you bind on earth shall be bound in Heaven." (Matthew 18:18)
- "How can anyone enter a strong man's house and carry off his possessions unless he first ties up the strong man?" (Matthew 12:29)

So if we bind a demon before casting it out it will have no power at all to cause any harm to anyone present.

One Example

A young lady I shall call Gloria brought her baby to be baptised by me. She came to Christ in the process and admitted her involvement in

57

spiritism and the occult. She also shared that she had sometimes been overtaken by trances. However, she wanted to be set free, and we soon made arrangements for her deliverance, which turned out to be over three full days. Several of us were involved in this, and my wife was led to fast. We were also shown that "through praise shall the victory come." As the evil spirits in Gloria reacted to our worship and manifested themselves we cast them out in Jesus' name. As each one left, Chris experienced an identical release in her own body. One of the demons would not move when commanded to in English but left rapidly when spoken to in a tongue!

By the third day we knew that Gloria was not completely free but were unsure about how to proceed. Someone said she might need cutting free from her ancestral line. Once we did this the way was opened for complete deliverance, though the demon pretended it wasn't there! Eventually I had a picture of a suitcase being shut down firmly and tightly locked, and the words "The case is closed." We all knew that it was, and praised the Lord for what He'd done.

Your Double Portion

Before we explore the other themes in our investigation, here is something a little different.

In the Old Testament there are seven recorded miracles of the prophet Elijah. Elisha is promised a double portion of Elijah's spirit (2 Kings 2:9–10), and there are fourteen recorded miracles of Elisha— twice as many, a double portion.

In the New Testament Jesus promises believers that when His Spirit comes they will do what He has been doing and even greater things (John 14:12). So, if you're a Christian, this is *your* "double portion". The following song from the Charismatic Renewal is based on John 14:12–14. There are no prizes for deciding Who is speaking the lyrics here!

"Truly, Truly I Say to You"

Truly, truly I say to you,
The works that I do shall believers do too,
And, because I am going to the Father for you,
Even greater things than these shall be done by you.

People will be saved and their spirits blessed,
Bodies will be healed and their minds at rest,
Wonders will be shown and my Name confessed
When you do the greater things that I've promised you.

People that are lost will return again,
Bodies that are sick will be freed from pain,
Spirits that are dry will be filled with rain
When you do the greater things that I've promised you.

Anything you ask will be given you,
Anything you need—it will come to you,
Everywhere you go I shall be there too
When you do the greater things that I've promised you.

Anything, everything I've promised you
You'll find will be there when My Spirit breaks through,
And, because I'm a righteous God and faithful and true,
I'll be there to give you strength for the things you do.

John Huggett, 1977

CHAPTER 8

Raise the Dead

Many Christians have no problem in recognising that believers have a part to play in raising people from the spiritual death of sin to newness of life in Christ. It's the Holy Spirit who convicts them and raises them, but, as we have seen, we are called to preach the Gospel to them and encourage them to repent and put their faith in Christ. This resurrection is enacted symbolically every time that someone is baptised in water using immersion (Romans 6:4).

But when Jesus told John the Baptist "the dead are raised", and commanded His disciples to "raise the dead", He was not meaning spiritual resurrection (Matthew 11:5 and Matthew 10:8). He was clearly instructing all His followers to raise to life people who are physically dead.

Who and When?

Obviously this happens to a comparatively low number of people—perhaps just hundreds compared with the billions who have become Christians. It also only happens when God decides it should, when the Holy Spirit leads people to expect it, and when they pray for it.

We are not thinking about near-death experiences, where people hover over their bodies and have beautiful experiences, and we are not only thinking about resuscitating people when their hearts have stopped. We are thinking about dead people either raised by believers in Jesus' Name, or dead people who return to life—either in answer to prayers, or because God sends them back in their physical bodies for a specific purpose. When

Jesus sent out His disciples on their own, knowing they had seen Him raise dead people, He commanded them all to raise the dead, and He never would have told them to unless He believed they could.

How and Why?

Occasionally an attempt to raise the dead has been unsuccessful. Before attempting to raise someone, at least one Christian present might be given a prophecy, a word of knowledge, or a Gift of Faith, a certainty that the dead person will rise (1 Corinthians 12:8-10). Any of these gifts of the Holy Spirit should then be confirmed by other believers and the circumstances. Sometimes persistent prayers have followed, or commands to the spirit of death to depart. All seven of the individuals raised in the Bible were either young or had died prematurely. This might be one of the reasons for a resurrection today.

The Example of Jesus

The three instances of Jesus raising people in the Gospels give some clues about this ministry.

First there was an only daughter who had just died, and whose father had requested the Lord to heal her. Jesus gave a command to her, "Get up!" And she did (Mark 5:22–23 and 35–43).

Then there was an only son who was on the way to his funeral. Jesus had compassion for the young man's widowed mother. Again He commanded, "Get up!" and he did. (Luke 7:11–17).

And there was an only brother who had been buried for four days. This time it was "for God's glory". Again the resurrection followed the command: "Lazarus, come out!" (John 11:1–44).

Early Resurrections

After Christ's resurrection the first people the Bible tells us who returned from the dead were some Old Testament saints, who apparently had heard what Jesus had done (Matthew 27:52).

Doctor Luke informs us that Peter raised Dorcas, a Christian lady who made robes and other garments (Acts 9:36–42). It's interesting that the apostle followed the exact procedure that Jesus had followed when raising Jairus' daughter. Observing Jesus then was part of Peter's training. So he put all the mourners out of the room to ensure there was a positive atmosphere. Then he commanded the dead woman to "get up" and helped her up. This led to spiritual revival there.

Luke also explains how Paul raised up Eutychus (Acts 20:7–12). This young man fell asleep during the apostle's long teaching at Midnight Communion. He fell from the third storey and was found to be dead. After Paul had raised him he went on to preach his sermon—as you do!

Through the Ages

As we have seen, after Christ's ascension some Christians continued to heal the sick, cast out demons, and work miracles for several centuries. And occasionally the dead were raised.

On Easter morning, AD 424, a brother and sister attended St Augustine's church at Hippo, in North Africa. They both suffered from convulsive seizures. Suddenly the young man fell down dead. He had no pulse and no life. But shortly afterwards he rose up again, completely normal and cured. Three days later, as people prayed, the same thing happened to his sister.

During the following centuries, we mainly know of people returning from the dead in spiritual revivals within different parts of the world—always Christian believers. These resurrections were among the signs and wonders which caused unbelievers to turn to Christ, and helped Christians to increase in faith, and consequently to expect greater things from God.

In 1850 a prosperous woman suffered from depression after the sudden death of her husband. Local Pastor Blumhardt gave her a room but she made several attempts at suicide. One day she locked her door and hung herself by the open window while the chambermaid was out. The pastor and a young man broke the door down and found her dead. They stayed with the body and quietly prayed. At length she was raised to life and was fully conscious. After that the woman became a devoted worker for the Lord under the leadership of Pastor Blumhardt.

The Early Twentieth Century

This was the period when some Pentecostals led the way in doing "greater things". Smith Wigglesworth, a Bradford plumber filled with the fire of the Holy Spirit, was a well-known healing evangelist in the first half of the century. He raised the dead on fourteen occasions.

Once a family was mourning the sad loss of a five-year-old boy. Wigglesworth was asked to pray with them. He requested the boy's father for the family to leave him alone in a locked room with the coffin. Wigglesworth then lifted the corpse of the boy from the coffin and stood it in the corner of the room. After this he rebuked death in the Name of Jesus and commanded it to surrender the boy. An amazing miracle happened: the child returned to life.

One night at ten o'clock, Wigglesworth was called out to a young lady dying of tuberculosis. He prayed from eleven o'clock until 3.30 am, when the lady died. He looked up at the window and saw a brilliant vision of Jesus. As he did, the colour came back into her face. She turned over and fell asleep. Next morning she played the piano and sang. Later it was found that her lungs, which had been in shreds before, had now been restored to a perfectly sound condition.

On another occasion Wigglesworth was asked to raise a corpse. He did, but the man was still suffering from the disease which had killed him. Wigglesworth told the family that unless they repented and put matters right within their home the man would die again. The family repented, Wigglesworth prayed for them, the man was healed and lived for thirty more years.

For physical resurrection the gift of discerning spirits may be essential (1 Corinthians 12:10). Doctor James Van Zyl, a healing evangelist in South Africa, raised the dead twice. Once, in response to hearing the Gospel, a man with severe asthma was walking to the front of the meeting when he suddenly collapsed on the floor. Doctor Van Zyl examined him and found he was dead. He commanded the spirit of death to leave. The dead man shook, revived, and then expired again.

This happened four times. Eventually the dead man revived completely. He got up, walked away, and was soon found to be healed, as well as "alive and kicking".

The other occasion was in another of Doctor Van Zyl's meetings. As he was preaching, there was a commotion. Everyone was turning, staring, and talking. An old lady had died in her seat. He again commanded the spirit of death to leave. The lady stood up, shook herself, and was found to be perfectly well. Once more a resurrection was a sign to unbelievers in the region.

One of the most remarkable instances concerns Mrs Zhang, of Shandong province, China, in 1904. She was converted through missionaries but was unable to interest her family in the Gospel. Six months later she contracted tuberculosis, and died one day at 3 pm. At sunset a noise was heard to be coming from the death chamber. She sat up in the grave clothes, alive.

She explained that she had been to Heaven, but God had told her to return to earth until the twelfth of the following month. In the next few weeks many people came to put their trust in Christ because of her outstanding testimony. Then, on the twelfth day of the following month, she calmly and deliberately put on her funeral clothes, lay down, and returned to Heaven.

Another resurrection occurred in China in the 1920s. American Pentecostal missionary Paul Dykstra had only been in the country for seven months when he fell ill with typhoid and double pneumonia. He became worse and worse, and at 6.30 one evening he passed away. Two doctors pronounced him dead. After fifteen minutes, one of the doctors, a Christian named Mrs Lawler, rebuked death in the Name of Jesus. Then he arose, but was disappointed after the glory of Heaven to be called back to earth. For over a week he lingered between life and death, but eventually realised God had more for him to do here, and he was then completely healed. He said, "As a result, in two villages afterwards 300 souls came from raw heathenism to the Lord .... Drug addicts were set free by the power of God, and the sick were healed."

At the First International Conference on Divine Healing, in Holland, there was a report about a woman around thirty years old who was a "Dorcas" to her church but who fell ill and died. She was visited by her Pastor Humberg and others who prayed for her. Eventually the pastor took her hand and raised her up in the Name of Jesus. She remembered nothing, but everyone rejoiced.

One night, Dorothy Hoare, a missionary to Japan, was called with a Japanese friend to the home of a seriously ill mother, but when they arrived she had passed away. Two doctors had examined her and left the death certificate. But Dorothy was convinced that it was not time for the lady to die. The missionary laid hands on the cold arm and prayed until she revived.

Agnes Sanford, in her book *Healing Light*, tells about a minister called on to baptise a dying baby. By the time the man arrived the child had been dead half an hour and was surrounded by weeping women. He laid hands on the child until his flesh began to grow warm. They continued with the baptismal service, and towards the end the child opened his eyes and was restored to his mother. Some sixteen years later, that child was a sturdy young man of seventeen and teaching in Sunday School.

In the same book Agnes told how a minister's child was born dead. The minister held up the lifeless form and prayed, "O God, if You give life to my child I'll dedicate both him and myself to Your service." His hands were placed on the child. The child breathed and lived.

In 1933, Ka Gi of China was about eleven years old when admitted to hospital with typhoid fever. He had several haemorrhages and lay for days unconscious. No more could be done for him medically. Ka Gi was pulseless, and breathing had stopped. But the Christian matron prayed all night for him. Early in the morning his little finger moved and his breathing started again. Ka Gi grew up and became a doctor, working in the hospital where he'd been raised up.

A black pastor in the Belgian Congo called Joshua had as a first convert the head of a secret society who renounced his old faith and burned his idols in public. This man later suffered a serious illness and was dying, but Joshua prayed for him and he was healed. But when Joshua got to his village he saw people digging a grave for forty-year-old Stephen, one of his elders. A group of relatives stood around where the dead body lay. Joshua called a few reliable Christians to come along and pray with him. Guided by the Holy Spirit they all suddenly found themselves definitely and audibly praying for Stephen to be raised up from the dead. After a period of prayer Stephen suddenly sat up, and he began taking off the grave clothes that bound him.

In 1933, a Christian lady wrote in a magazine about how the Lord showed her she would soon die. A few days later she had a bad attack of bronchitis, which grew rapidly worse. When her pastor and others visited her, she tried to say, "Rebuke death," but her tongue was paralysed. Eventually her body became rigid and cold, her eyes sunk into her head and she passed away. After a while the pastor *did* rebuke death, and an intense battle followed against evil forces, together with intercessory prayer. Suddenly she came back to life. She told how she had seen the gates of the New Jerusalem but was unable to enter in. But she saw Jesus standing, and, as she pronounced His Name, she felt a flow of life through her whole body. As she revived she realised that all the pain she had previously suffered was gone. She lived a normal life again. She became a missionary in China and later returned to live in the north of England.

In 1937, Lindsay Glegg, a well-known speaker at the Keswick Convention, introduced there a minister who told how his three-year-old son had succumbed to a disease which baffled the specialist. While the family doctor was visiting, the boy died. The minister said, "Bring me hot blankets." For nine hours he and his wife cradled their son and prayed. At Keswick the minister said, "My boy's now twenty, and at college, and doing a wonderful work for Christ."

When a thirty-eight-year-old Chinese drunkard, Dae Sia Long, died in Thailand, Pastor Lee knew the man was not ready to go, and he cried to the Lord that the man's life should return. He spoke into the man's ears, "Confess your sins and God will forgive you." The body was still stiff, but the dead man's tongue began to move, and tears ran from his eyes. He became alive and normal in appearance. On the Sunday morning he attended Pastor Lee's church with his wife and family. Sometime later, Dr Harvey McAlister of New York met the former dead man at a service in Formosa (Taiwan). While he was there he witnessed over thirty deaf and dumb people healed.

The Later Twentieth Century

Even before the Charismatic Movement, in 1954, some clergy were demanding to know why the Church of England was not training people to obey the *whole* commission of Christ. The Rev F L Wyman, Rector of St Paul's, York, asked that as by then "Heal the sick" was fast becoming part of the Church's ministry, would it not be consistent to follow *all* the other missionary commands as well, including "Raise the dead?" (Some of the examples I have given are from his book *The Dead are Raised Up*.) He added, "The Church's programme is, for the most part, far too ineffective and powerless to cause serious anxiety to Satan's plans."

Once the renewal got under way it was not long before there were reports of resurrections, as well as resuscitations. During the Indonesian revival of 1965 water was turned into wine for communion purposes, Christians walked on water to reach an otherwise inaccessible island with the Gospel, and people were raised from the dead. This was witnessed by independent journalists. Rev David Pawson later told nine hundred Evangelicals at Morecambe that the supernatural events that had taken place in Indonesia were examples of John 14:12 in action.

More of my examples of raising the dead are from David Pytches' book *Come, Holy Spirit*. Among those raised up in Indonesia was a nine-year-old boy who collapsed and died at the beginning of a meeting. Five hours later the evangelist Saul arrived. The Lord said to him, "Blow into the boy's mouth and nose and put your hand on his forehead." Saul obeyed, and, after fifteen minutes, there was movement. Sometime later the boy was fully conscious.

A twenty-five-year-old illiterate girl named Anna became a highly gifted Christian. She was used to evangelise and to heal both the blind and the deaf. Once she was led to pray for a two-year-old child who had died. After she had prayed for him he was raised up like Jairus' daughter.

Mother Sharon was also illiterate. She brought a child back to life that had been dead for six hours. The Scriptures were read, and, when she had finished praying, the child's life returned. Another child had been dead two days already. Ants were crawling over its eyes and body. Instead of the tropical custom of burying the child on the first day, the parents called Mother Sharon. She arrived two days later, and, after a time of prayer, the child was restored to life.

Kurt Koch wrote an exciting report of the revival in Indonesia. A pastor told him of two other people on a neighbouring island. After they had died, their bodies were both carried out of the hospital in which they had been patients, but, after prayer, they had both come back to life.

Paul Yonggi Cho was speaking at a meeting when he received a call from his wife: "Come home, your son is dying." Samuel was one of eight schoolboys who had already died after eating deep-fried silkworms sold by a street vendor in South Korea. When he'd known he was dying, he'd said, "Tell Daddy to pray for me—but I'm pretty sure I'm going to Heaven tonight." But Cho cried, "Father, I will not let my boy go!" He prayed for forgiveness for everything he could think of, while picturing his son as alive, strong, and healthy. Eventually he thundered, "Samuel, in the Name of Jesus Christ of Nazareth, rise up and walk!" The boy sprang to his feet, alive. Then he told how he had seen Jesus, who had allowed him to return.

Jean Darnell, in *Heaven, Here I Come*, told how her mother informed her pastor that she was going to die that day. Later a male nurse told Jean, who was aged fifteen, that her mother had died. In spite of discouragement from the pastor, Jean prayed constantly: "Bring my mother back to me." Eventually, her eyelids fluttered and her lips moved. "Why did you bring me back?" she asked. At this stage the doctor diagnosed a major heart attack. But she gradually recovered. Her mother said she'd been to heaven, but Jesus said, "I have to take you back."

Kath Clark, of the South American Missionary Society, told how, in a spiritually dry part of Chile, Evangelist Andres Montupal heard of a very ill girl in her early teens who had just died. He arrived at her home to find her cold and stiff, and her mother weeping terribly. With others he prayed twice, but nothing happened. The third time he prayed, "Lord, for Your glory, so that these people may know You exist and have power, raise their daughter." At this the girl coughed, moved, and showed clear signs of life. The family came to know the Lord and a church was formed. Kath subsequently met the girl and family when she visited the church.

In 1982, Captain R E Wilbourne told how, when he was a Church Army student, he fell ill with pneumonia and pleurisy and was rushed to hospital. It was in the days before we have the drugs of today. His relatives came to see him, but he was certified dead and taken to the mortuary. He told of his experience of life in Heaven. Eventually he heard a voice crying, "Don't let him die!" It was his landlady. He then felt he was falling through space and back onto the mortuary slab. He asked the attendant where he was, to the latter's horror! He had been dead for three hours.

During 1984 Ron Skele told how Brother Alexander, a largely uneducated man, was leading a meeting in Zaire when the corpse of a young woman was carried in and her fiancé challenged him defiantly: "You say God raises people from the dead. Here's a test for you." The woman had been dead four days, and there was an unbearable stench in the room. Alexander called the little congregation together, and they lifted their hands and praised God, rejoicing for twenty minutes.

Suddenly Alexander felt someone tugging at his jacket. The woman who had been dead was standing among them, eyes closed, hands raised, and praising God. When the remainder of the congregation saw her, they bolted out of the door, with Alexander in hot pursuit. The miracle shook the whole area, and people turned to the Lord in large numbers.

In the later years of the twentieth century, a number of people reported at meetings, in books, online, and in videos that they had been to Heaven. These had enjoyed something of the glory but were then sent back or found themselves back on earth. Later they shared similar things, such as the beauty of the music and the colours and meeting their loved ones. Not one of them wished to return here, because all their Heavenly experiences were so wonderful.

Recent Resurrections

In the twenty-first century Canon Andrew White, former vicar of the Anglican church in Baghdad, Iraq, reported three raisings from the dead that had occurred during his unique Middle East ministry.

Currently there is revival in Algeria and parts of North Africa, with many Moslems coming to Christ. The largest evangelistic crusades worldwide are at this moment probably those of *Christ for All Nations*, led first by Reinhard Bonnke and then Daniel Kolenda. In spite of persecution they have held Gospel campaigns throughout the African continent and other countries. For over thirty years the huge, now open-air meetings have been attended by hundreds of thousands of people. Eighty million have registered their decision to follow Christ and thousands have been healed. Following the many healings and miracles, attendance has swelled on subsequent days, so it's not surprising that reports of resurrections have come from these situations too. Recently a baby died in the complex at the close of one of the huge gatherings, but it was brought back to life in the Name of Jesus. This was witnessed by onlookers at the scene.

The only person I know of who has been called by God to specialise in raising people from the dead is David Hogan. Over forty years he and his team have brought about 500 people back to life in the North American continent. Many of these have been younger people and babies. Thank You, Jesus.

CHAPTER 9

Freely Give

" **F**reely you have received, freely give."
This outreach command of Jesus in Matthew 10:8 has often headed a sermon about financial giving, but it's not just about money. Certainly the principle of Christians giving away all or part of what they have received is true of finances. Believers can set an example to others in the area of tithes and offerings. During the second century AD, pagan temples expected to receive offerings if they gave healing, but Christian churches would not charge for healing, out of sheer love for Jesus.

When Jesus sent out His disciples, He told them not to worry about taking material things with them (verses 9–10). They were to rely on their hosts for provision, not waste time with those unwilling to receive their message or ministry—not to throw pearls to pigs (Matthew 7:6). Jesus was concerned that everything else was subservient to the main purpose of the mission—preaching the gospel— so this last of Christ's outreach commands in this passage should be seen in the light of this.

Receiving and Giving

If we look at the command in its context, we see that it refers to the preceding ones. The disciples freely received the Gospel from Jesus, and they would freely give it. Peter's mother-in-law had been healed by the Lord, and Peter would bring healing to other sick people. Nathanael had benefited by a word of knowledge from Jesus, and perhaps Nathanael could bring a word of knowledge to someone else. What Jesus had freely given to them, they would freely share.

Once at the Beautiful Gate of the Temple Peter said to the lame man, "What I have I give you" (Acts 3:6). This is what Christ expects from His Church today. Out of gratitude for what He has done for us, and concern for others in need, we are freely to share what He has given us.

Spiritual Gifts

The Bible mentions many natural gifts that God has given. St Paul lists some functional gifts for the Church (Romans 12:4–7), leadership gifts (Ephesians 4:11–13), and ministry gifts (1 Corinthians 12:28–31). But I'm going to concentrate in this chapter on the only ones that Paul calls *spiritual* gifts, those supernatural ones in 1 Corinthians 12:8–10:

> To one there is given through the Spirit the message of wisdom, to another the message of knowledge by means of the same Spirit, to another faith by the same Spirit, to another gifts of healing by that one Spirit, to another miraculous powers, to another prophecy, to another distinguishing between spirits, to another speaking in different kinds of tongues, to another the interpretation of tongues.

Paul lists these nine gifts parallel to the nine fruits he lists in Galatians 5:22–23. He could also have added dreams, visions (Acts 2:17), and revelations (1 Corinthians 14:26).

Why Are These So Relevant?

Why have I chosen these gifts to explore in this investigation of Christ's outreach commands?

- The supernatural ministries that Christ ordered are best aided by these supernatural gifts.

- The majority of people who see frequent healings have usually manifested one or more of these.
- These are neglected by many Christian people but often because of misunderstandings.
- Our own ministry would not have been so fruitful if we had not drawn upon these gifts.

These gifts will provide heat, light and sound for the Church that wants to outreach for Jesus. The ones that add sound to a situation are prophecy, tongues and interpretation of tongues. Ones that throw light on a situation are words of knowledge and wisdom and discernment. Ones that bring heat to a situation are gifts of faith and healing and the working of miracles. We need tools for the garden, we need *these* tools to be fruitful in winning people to Christ.

The most important of these spiritual gifts seems to be prophecy (1 Corinthians 14:1). The most recorded in the Bible is the word or message of knowledge. The most misunderstood is undoubtedly speaking in tongues. The most neglected generally is the working of miracles. And probably the most needed in this country at the moment is distinguishing between spirits, so that more Christians are not led astray by the subtle wiles of the devil (Ephesians 6:11–13).

Goodbye to Cessationism

Before we explore the gifts in a little more detail, there's a good reason why many church leaders—and therefore their fellowships—ignore these gifts or leave them to other churches. At the start of the twentieth century, most people in the UK had had no personal experience of miracles, and it was assumed by the majority that they could not be expected to occur again—though some students of Church history acknowledged that they had happened in past revivals.

Theologians at that time had various ideas about the reasons for the absence of these miracles. Some liberal scholars proposed that the early Church had invented them. More conservative ones believed the Bible accounts but said that miracles stopped after the last of the original apostles died (John, around AD 100). However, when others noticed that divine healings, miracles, signs and wonders and spiritual gifts continued for several centuries after Christ's ascension, most decided that they ceased when the Bible was completed. Then, they said, these things were no longer required to confirm the truth of the Gospel (as in Mark 16:20). This theory of cessationism was popularised by B B Warfield in 1918.

It was also said that the book of Acts reflected a transitional period, like a rocket to get the Church off the ground. Once it was "up and running" there was no need of supernatural gifts, for example, to use in the churches. They pointed to where St Paul wrote that prophecies, tongues and knowledge would cease (1 Corinthians 13:8). But there he is referring to "when perfection comes" and when "I shall know fully, even as I am fully known" (verses 10–12)—in Heaven.

But most Christians thereafter carried on as they had before, not expecting the miraculous. Emphasis was on what Jesus *used* to do, and that He could do these things because He was God's Son. However, as the twentieth century progressed, so did the louder voice of faith. First through the Pentecostals, then the Charismatics, as well as through others in parts of the world where they had never heard of either, there came reports and confirmation of miracles, and of God working in modern times using supernatural as well as natural means. I have given just a comparatively few examples in this investigation. Even if only one of these was correct, it would cancel the theory of cessationism. That is erroneous and now completely discredited.

Unfortunately, many people do not realise this, and even some preachers that do, as I wrote earlier, say they are not cessationists but act as though they are. Perhaps they prefer to stay in their comfort zone of ignoring greater things that not only the Lord but what they might do. I pray that more leaders will expect great things *from* God and attempt great things *for* God.

The Origin of the Gifts

The Bible says that these gifts are bestowed by God the Holy Spirit (1 Corinthians 12:11) at the will of God the Father (Hebrews 2:4) for the glory of God the Son (John 16:14). They are all given by Almighty

God (Galatians 3:5) to any Christian believer who asks for them (1 Corinthians 14:1) and who acts by faith to apply them (e.g. Acts 2:4).

Who Can Have These Gifts?

You can if you are a Christian: "Earnestly desire the spiritual gifts" (1 Corinthians 14:1). Paul writes this even to people who have misused such gifts, for he regards them as very valuable. Do not be distracted by the fact that some believers like those Corinthians have abused these gifts. Father Dennis Bennett wisely told us, "The cure for abuse is not *dis*use but *right* use."

A misunderstanding has arisen by taking 1 Corinthians 12 verse 11 "He gives them to each one just as He determines", without noticing the important first verse of 1 Corinthians 14, addressed by Paul to *all* the church members in the city of Corinth: "Eagerly desire spiritual gifts."

These gifts are completely different from natural gifts. You have a natural gift either because you were born with it or because you've learned a skill. You have a spiritual gift not only if God decides to give it but if you have sought for it, asked for it, and trusted Him to use it. Do not think that because someone is spiritually gifted you cannot have the same gift that they have. All these gifts are available to you, a treasure chest of manifestations.

How to Receive a Gift

Years ago, someone said to me, "John, I believe you'd benefit from speaking in tongues."

At the time, I immediately replied, "If God wants to give me that gift, He will."

But I find that it doesn't always work like that. God did not give me the gift of eternal life out of the blue. I first had to repent of my sins and put my trust in Christ. Likewise, to receive the gift of tongues, I had to trust Him to fill me with His Spirit. You may find yourself manifesting a spiritual gift when it is needed as you pray with someone, or you may have to ask the Lord for a particular gift if you sense your need of it.

At one time I'd often shared a word of knowledge when ministering healing or giving prayer counselling in private, but I realised how beneficial this gift could be in a meeting, so I asked the Lord to give it to me at one, and decided to trust Him for the appropriate words.

What happens if you ask God for a particular gift is that He may soon put you in a position where you are going to need it. So don't ask the Lord for the gift of working miracles unless you are prepared to act on it, or you'll soon have to work a miracle!

Soon after I had asked for the word of knowledge in public I was leading a Healing Prayer Service near Nottingham, and there had been queues for the laying-on-of-hands. Chris suddenly felt her breath being taken away and her hands shaking violently. Immediately I shared a word of knowledge: "There is a lady here who is deeply hurt inside. She needs ministry but has not come forward to receive it." An elderly lady shuffled forward, crying. My wife ministered to her with words of comfort and prayer for the deep hurts inside her.

After the service some people told us, "You wouldn't know this because you are just visitors here, but if anyone needed prayer ministry it was definitely that lady. A few weeks ago, her husband walked to their garden shed, took some weed killer, and committed suicide."

A Postman Too

The other main misunderstanding about spiritual gifts concerns the way they operate—again quite differently from natural gifts. If you are good at painting landscapes or playing the violin, we say that's your gift, your talent, or your skill. It belongs to you personally. But spiritual gifts do not belong to any one individual: they belong to Christ and His Church. They are not permanent possessions but momentary manifestations (1 Corinthians 12:7). They are not owned by a Christian but given by God the Holy Spirit *as and when needed*.

An old riddle may help here: "When is a fruit tree a postman too?"

Answer: "When it's a Christian who manifests both the fruit and the gifts of the Holy Spirit."

The fruit tree is self-explanatory, and the postman too (or postwoman) is an excellent example of how the supernatural gifts operate. The postman collects a gift from the sorting office and carries it to the address on the envelope or packet, then delivers it to the person it's intended for. At no time does the postman *own* the gift. He is simply the agent who passes it on to someone. In the same way a spiritual gift is not normally for a Christian to keep but to pass on. It's mainly intended for the person or group of people that the Lord wants it to be shared with.

I have a *ministry* of healing—which I think is the best translation of 1 Corinthians 12:28—because the Lord has called me frequently to minister to sick and needy people. But at this point in time I do not have a *gift* of healing (verse 9). In fact, I do not know I've had one until it's *gone* from me. It's only when someone tells me that a person has been healed after I have prayed for them that I realise that I've manifested the gift. The word of wisdom is another gift you may not know you've shared until someone listening tells you. Other gifts are more obvious, but we are not to boast about *having* them—just to *share* them!

I believe church leaders should encourage people to share such gifts at appropriate points, in church and elsewhere. Some church leaders ask their members who already are given gifts in advance of the Sunday service, to inform them just before it, so that everything is done "in a fitting and orderly way" (1 Corinthians 14:40). Whatever the procedure, true Charismatic worship is not always just singing one worship song after another—great though that is, as it enables us to uplift the Lord and keep our eyes on Him. If instead a time of silence arises between the songs, we may wait on the Lord to see if He'll speak through the gifts.

The Purpose of the Gifts

Those who ignore these gifts may not realise their value. The Bible gives two main reasons:

- *They can help to* edify *the Church (1 Corinthians 14:12).* We need building up, encouragement, strength, and help from one another, to grow in the Christian life. The Bible can aid this, and so can spiritual gifts. Ones that can particularly do this in the context of *worship* are prophecy, tongues and interpretation, discernment, and words of knowledge and wisdom.

- *They can help to* extend *the Church (Acts 8:6–7).* We have already seen that signs and wonders, which are aided by these gifts, can both confirm the truth of the Gospel and attract unbelievers to hear it. Ones that can particularly do this, especially in the context of *witness,* are gifts of faith, healing, and miracles, which we've seen produce fastest-growing churches.

Guidance and the Gifts

When the Bible was completed, God did not decide to stop speaking in other ways! He speaks for example through Scripture, conscience, nature, other people (especially Christians), books, letters, films, discs, online information, angels, visions, dreams, supernatural revelations, physical anointings, doors opening and closing, everyday circumstances, and the inward witness of the Holy Spirit (1 John 5:10). To this list we can confidently add the spiritual gifts, and not just in church, for in both the Bible and today's world God has spoken like this to His children in their everyday lives.

Since 1975 He has gently thumped Chris in the stomach whenever He wants to talk to us, which He does practically everywhere we go. This is part of our fellowship with Him. This two-way communication is brought out in some hymns:

"O let me *hear Thee speaking* in accents clear and still,"
and in songs:
"He walks with me and *talks* with me along life's narrow way."

"And He walks with me and He *talks* with me and He tells me I am His own."

The Important Gift of Prophecy

The apostle Paul not only encouraged the Christians at Corinth especially to seek the gift of prophecy (1 Corinthians 14:1), but said, "You can all prophesy in turn" (verse 31). It's clear from this and elsewhere that he's not referring to prophets like those in the Old Testament, nor to preaching, though this might sometimes be included in a prophecy. The sermon usually has to be prepared. The prophecy, however, is usually spontaneous, though occasionally someone may be given words from the Holy Spirit to pass on to someone else when the two next meet up.

Paul is writing about ordinary believers being sometimes given direct words from God about a particular situation, to be contributed at an appropriate point, especially when Christians are gathered, like the postman delivering the letter. This is what I understand by the gift of prophecy, and when the same believer keeps manifesting this gift he or she may be referred to as a prophet.

Jesus told us to beware of false prophets, recognising them by their fruits (Matthew 7:15–20), meaning not just the results of their prophecies but their manner of life (Galatians 5:22–23). However, once again, since Pentecost any Christian might manifest this gift. I've found that, when I do, it can be like opening a packet of tissues. Just a few words may come at first. Then, as I trust the Holy Spirit for more, He gives me more until the flow of words suddenly stops.

These contemporary prophecies usually bring one or more of either encouragement, guidance, exhortation or challenge. Sometimes they predict what will happen, in which case whether they are correct will be confirmed by whether they come to pass. But most prophecies simply relay a message from God. It's reckoned that perhaps 20 per cent of prophecies are *fore*telling and 80 per cent *forth* telling. Jesus is looking for those who will step out in faith to prophesy (Romans 12:6).

Chris and I were once leading a week's healing mission at a Pentecostal church in Market Drayton, Shropshire. One evening I spoke out a prophecy that the Lord was giving me, that He would reveal actual names and addresses of the people for whom the local Christians were to pray. As I said these words the pastor of that church heard in his mind the names and address of two people he had never come across. It turned out that there was indeed an elderly couple with that name and address living eight miles away at Newport. That week the pastor visited them in their home. He talked with them about Jesus and invited them to come to his church. The following Sunday they did come, and both soon surrendered their lives to Christ.

Speaking in Tongues and Interpretation

Speaking in tongues—in a language you have not learned (Mark 16:17)—is frequently the first supernatural gift a Christian receives (Acts 19:6). It's a precious gift of God that is valuable and powerful, sometimes described as a love language. Some people have described it as like a barrier being unplugged from deep inside them, enabling a release of power (John 7:37–39).

Yet I've never heard so many excuses for rejecting or ignoring this particular gift:

- "It's a psychological fantasy."
- "It was just for Bible times."
- "It's what those odd Pentecostals do."
- "It's for baby Christians, not mature ones."
- "It can cause division in churches."
- "It's the least of the gifts, for Paul puts it last on his list."

However, some people genuinely misunderstand the gift. They quote out of context "Do all speak in tongues?" where Paul obviously expects the answer "no" (1 Corinthians 12:30). But there he's writing about a *message* in tongues. Tongues is another gift available to every believer. So who can speak in tongues? Canon Michael Harper came to this conclusion: "All *may*, many *do*, some *should*."

Such misunderstandings are often due to confusing the three main uses of the gift of tongues:

- *As a sign.* It's a clear indication that at one time someone has been baptised in the Spirit: "There could be no doubt about it, for they heard them speaking in tongues and praising God" (Acts 10:46—Living Bible). It can also be the gateway to the other supernatural gifts.

80

- *As a language for prayer and praise* (1 Corinthians 14:2). The Holy Spirit gives us the exact words we need to say to God. He understands them if we do not, so it's particularly useful when we do not know how to pray (Romans 8:26). And, because we are praying with our *spirits*, our mouths are free to say or sing what we do not normally understand, and our minds are free to picture the Lord or the person(s) we are praying for (1 Corinthians 14:15).

- *As a message* (1 Corinthians 14:13). This must be interpreted (not translated) in the usual language understood by the hearers so that they can be edified (1 Corinthians 14:12). The interpretation is usually conveyed by particular Christians, and when this follows a tongue the two gifts are companions, equivalent in value to prophecy (verse 5). The tongue is like a red traffic light. We then wait in silence for the green light of interpretation to follow.

When someone first speaks in tongues the "dentist's text" is appropriate: "Open your mouth wide and I will fill it" (Psalm 81:10). But you cannot just open your mouth like a goldfish! You need to speak, but not in your usual language, then trust God to turn it into the real thing.

After the initial filling you have complete control over speaking in tongues (1 Corinthians 14:32). It's like a radio. You can decide when to "switch on" and "switch off" and turn up the volume. The only thing you have no control over is the programme. That is given by God the Holy Spirit (Acts 2:4). And He will not give you a snake if you ask for a fish! (Matthew 7:10). So Paul wrote,

- "I want you all to speak in tongues" (1 Corinthians 14:5)
- "Do not forbid speaking in tongues" (verse 39).
- "Do not put out the Spirit's fire" (1 Thessalonians 5:19).

Messages of Knowledge and Wisdom

Supernatural knowledge may come in words that are self-explanatory or need explanation, in pictures that may need to be described, in fleeting impressions or convictions, in revelations seen with the eyes of the mind (1 Corinthians 14:26 and 30), in visions seen with the eyes of the body (Acts 2:17), in feelings manifested through the body, or by the action of angels (Hebrews 1:14). The knowledge may arrive out of the blue, as we are waiting on the Lord in prayer or silence, or as we minister or are being ministered to. It's then up to us to speak it out when we have opportunity.

Supernatural wisdom may be the ability to apply the knowledge. Jesus also used it to shame His enemies. When they watched to see if He would heal on the Sabbath, He asked them, "Which is lawful on the Sabbath: to do good or to do evil, to save life or to kill?" (Mark 3:4).

Sometimes He gives someone a "nudge" to manifest such gifts, and it may not be until the Christian speaks out that the purpose of God's guidance becomes clear. A lady at Hull that I'll call Shirley asked her vicar to pray that she'd receive words of knowledge. Not long afterwards I was leading a healing mission for twelve Anglican parishes in that area, and Shirley told me of her desire.

"I feel it could be so useful in guiding me to pray with sick people," she shared. Then in the Sunday morning service prayer ministry time Shirley cried, "John, I'm suddenly feeling a trembling on my lips and hands, and I've pain in my chest!"

She could not understand it, but I said, "It's the answer to your prayer. The Lord is anointing your lips for speaking and your hands for touching."

"What about my chest pains?" she asked.

"Perhaps you are meant to minister to someone with chest trouble," I explained.

Sure enough, when Shirley asked the man sitting next to her what he needed prayer for, he replied, "I have chest pains." So, having gained the vicar's permission, she laid hands on the man for healing.

Distinguishing between Spirits

When Christians are uncertain about someone's motivation and the Bible does not clarify this (Acts 17:11), our recommendation is, "If you're not sure, *share!*" And sometimes the best person to share with is a

Christian known to be used in discerning of spirits (1 Corinthians 12:10). George Fox, founder of the Quakers (when they actually quaked in the Spirit!), explained, "The Lord has given me a Spirit of Discerning, by which I many times saw the states and conditions of people and could try their spirits whether they were of God."

We may need to know whether someone requires healing or deliverance. Sometimes it is both (Luke 13:11–13). We may also need to discern which evil spirit has gained a hold upon someone, such as infirmity (Luke 13:11) or divination (Acts 16:16). And sometimes discerning a spiritual diagnosis can make all the difference. A man was in a psychiatric hospital for fifty-two years, but a Christian psychiatrist set him free from demons, and he left in his right mind!

Gifts of Healing

No one has the automatic right to set themselves up as a healer without recognition. Most Christians who have manifested gifts or ministries of healing (1 Corinthians 12:8 and 28) started by simply obeying Jesus' outreach command, praying and trusting Him to cure sick people. Many of them found that He honoured their faith by answering their prayers.

How do you know if you have a ministry of healing? There are only two certain evidences: when people keep getting healed through you and when others keep telling you this. If you believe God is calling you to conduct a *public* healing ministry, you will need to ask your pastor whether this is possible in your church or if it's for elsewhere. You may find that your gift is associated with a particular area of healing. For example, some people have a specific ministry to backs, others to knees, and so on.

The Gift of Faith and Working of Miracles

The Gift of Faith is not saving faith (Ephesians 2:8–9), increasing faith (Luke 17:5), or the fruit of faith (which also translates as faithfulness— Galatians 5:22). It's an inrush of faith for a particular purpose, such as

83

an instant healing or a miracle, and is often required before any of these. When it's in operation, the Christian concerned has no doubt that God is going to do what he is commanding in Jesus' Name, and often that He's going to do it then.

As with all of these gifts, it's essential if you have this faith to speak it out at the right time. When a lady with a stick came to me for prayer, I knew she wouldn't need it again. When I told her, she was hesitant, saying, "I've needed it for eight years!" But eventually she let go of it and left it in the church. One church had a room for discarded sticks!

Working miracles is of course not magic. It's usually the ability to do things that cannot be achieved by natural means. Some things that appear to us miraculous may be taken for granted by our descendants.

- One kind of miracle is *multiplication.* Jesus can make a little food go a long way. He can do the same with a little money or a little petrol or whatever is needed.
- Another miracle that happens today is *re-creation,* when He re-creates new parts for people's bodies.
- A different miracle is *transportation,* when a Christian is suddenly transported many miles in a few seconds, perhaps to help someone in need (cf. Acts 8:40).

Matthew 15:31 in the Living Bible tells of several miracles:

> What a spectacle it was! Those who hadn't been able to say a word were talking excitedly, and those with missing arms and legs had new ones; the crippled were walking and jumping around, and those who had been blind were gazing about them! The crowds just marvelled, and praised the God of Israel.

Aliss Cresswell of Chester, joint leader of Morning Star Europe, is an international speaker, business woman and "miracle worker", who constantly works miracles in the Name of Jesus in her daily life and work. Aliss is a normal Christian who has been given this ministry, but the gift is available to be used occasionally by every believer.

The Bible states,

> "Is anything too hard for the Lord?" (Genesis 18:14)

> "Nothing is too difficult for You." (Jeremiah 32:17)

> "With God all things are possible." (Matthew 19:26)

> "Everything is possible for him who believes." (Mark 9:23)

CHAPTER 10

Be Filled with the Spirit

harp readers will have noticed straightaway that this is not an outreach command of Christ. It could not be, for the Holy Spirit did not come to stay with the Church until Jesus returned to His Father (John 16:7). The reason I make this the climax of this investigation in this last chapter is because it's a big open secret—some would say *the* big open secret—of effective outreach. It's a scriptural command given by St Paul to all the Christians at Ephesus, and is in the present imperative continuous tense, meaning "Keep getting filled with the Spirit" (Ephesians 5:18). Paul contrasts this with being drunk with wine (some of you may have had the experience of being "drunk in the Spirit"—cf. Acts 2:13).

Training courses on evangelism come thick and fast among the Evangelicals and can be very useful. But I have known some which lay stress on what a struggle it can be to witness, yet no mention was made of the big open secret. Get filled with the Spirit, Christian, and you *will* be bold (Acts 4:31). Trust Him also to show you what to say and He *will* (Matthew 10:19–20).

Word and Spirit

If someone is truly speaking by the Holy Spirit, what is said will never contradict the Bible. But problems can arise if an Evangelical leader insists that the Spirit speaks *only* through the Bible, or those who expound it. They can also arise if a charismatic leader is not grounded in God's written word.

International Bible teacher Doctor R T Kendall has encountered many *Word* churches, that emphasise the Bible, and *Spirit* churches that emphasise the Holy Spirit. I, like him, would love to see more Word *and* Spirit churches. This chapter is about the Holy Spirit and our experiences of Him, but we cannot make spiritual progress by just living on past experiences, however wonderful (nor second-hand ones). We must also explore what the *Bible* says about the fullness of the Spirit.

Power at Pentecost

John the Baptist had prophesied of Christ: "He will baptise you with the Holy Spirit and with fire" (Matthew 3:11). In John chapters 14–16, Jesus promises His disciples that the Spirit will be their Helper in all sorts of ways. He adds, "He lives *with* you and will be *in* you" (John 14:17). This came to pass on the first Easter Sunday evening, when the risen Christ appeared to ten of them. Then "He breathed on them and said, 'Receive the Holy Spirit'" (John 20:22). This is not "John's version of Pentecost". No way would a disciple who was present on that powerful occasion confuse it with the very different peaceful circumstances on Easter Sunday evening. When St John writes about this he's referring to the *indwelling* of the Spirit, that happens today when someone is *born* of the Spirit. This may have no outward sign from God.

When St Luke writes of receiving the Spirit he's referring to the *filling*, accompanied by a manifest sign. He states that before Christ's ascension Jesus says, "In a few days you will be baptised with the Holy Spirit" (Acts 1:5). Then comes a different preposition: "You will receive power when the Holy Spirit comes *upon* you" (verse 8). We are not told that the 120 people at Pentecost were *born* of the Spirit — they were already believers. Instead, this was the *Baptism* in the Spirit that Jesus had promised, the initial conscious overflow of power in their Christian lives, accompanied by speaking in tongues.

It was not the 120 who needed to repent and believe after Peter's sermon but the multitude (Acts 2:38). Traditionalists say Baptism in (or by) the Spirit in 1 Corinthians 12:13 means regeneration, but I believe it does not. By the time St Paul wrote that letter it seemed usual to encourage someone to receive the Spirit in a definite way *after* they became a Christian (Acts 8:14–19; Acts 19:1–7). Although this powerful experience sometimes happens at the same time as new birth (Acts 10:44–46), it's a conscious experience with a manifest sign (Acts 19:6) — regeneration usually is not.

Doctor R A Torrey, sidekick of evangelist D L Moody, once said that he'd met many people who were born of the Spirit and didn't know when it had happened, while he had never met any Christian who'd been baptised in the Spirit who could not remember it.

Why Be Filled? Speak Up!

In Acts 6:3, Luke calls the fullness of the Spirit a qualification for a good deacon, naming several people including Stephen, who was known for his boldness and wisdom in speaking to hostile Jews and working signs and wonders (verse 5). Every mention of being filled in the New Testament is connected with *speaking*. The key verse is Acts 1, verse 8: "You shall receive (dynamite) power when the Holy Spirit comes upon you, and you shall be My witnesses." A witness is someone who *says* what he or she has seen. After Pentecost, each time the Bible states that someone was filled with the Holy Spirit, they immediately opened their mouth and spoke (or sang)—either *to* the Lord or *for* the Lord.

There are several references to being filled in Acts as well as the one in Ephesians 5:18–19, which is an example of being filled to speak *to* God: "Be filled with the Spirit, speaking to one another with psalms, hymns, and songs in the Spirit." Other references are of being filled to speak *for* God, such as Acts 4:8: "Peter, filled with the Holy Spirit, said to them ..."

Doctor Luke in Acts 9:17 tells how Paul was baptised in the Spirit: "Ananias ... said, 'Brother Saul, the Lord Jesus ... has sent me so that you may see again and be filled with the Holy Spirit.'" No manifestation is mentioned in that particular instance, but we know that St Paul wrote some years later, "I thank God that I speak in tongues more than all of you" (1 Corinthians 14:18).

Other references in the New Testament to receiving the Spirit do not mention being filled, but it's the same experience, for most of them are not just describing regeneration but an outpouring accompanied by a conscious visible manifestation.

I was once preparing a teenage girl for Confirmation. When I mentioned being filled with the Spirit, she said, "Oh, I don't need that. I already witness at school."

"That's great," I said, "but can you say, like Peter, 'I cannot help speaking about what I've seen and heard?'" (Acts 4:20).

"Oh no," she cried. "Perhaps I do need to be filled after all!"

Soon afterwards she spoke in tongues.

Life in the Spirit

Sometimes people confuse being filled with the Spirit with walking (or living) in the Spirit. It may help if we remember that different Bible terms are associated with different experiences.

- *Born of the Spirit* (John 3:5) is associated with *salvation*—it's new birth.
- *Walking (or living) in the Spirit* (Galatians 5:16 and 25) is especially associated with *sanctification*—with becoming more holy, more victorious, and more like Jesus in character.
- *Filled with the Spirit* (Acts 2:4) is especially associated with *service*, particularly *speaking*, so that we obey His commands through worshipping and witnessing.

Of course, some things overlap, and we should not grieve the sensitive Spirit (Ephesians 4:30) by limiting Him (John 3:34) or quenching Him by obstructing His work (1 Thessalonians 5:19). But the distinctions help to explain why it is possible for a Christian to be baptised in the Spirit and manifest gifts without showing much evidence of the fruit of the Spirit in their life. In contrast, many Christians who express the fruit of the Spirit never manifest the supernatural gifts.

As we saw earlier, Spirit-filled believers may be no better than others. Millions of Christians who have not had the Baptism in the

Spirit have loved and served Christ faithfully. The Baptism in the Spirit means to be better empowered and better equipped to serve the Lord more effectively. We can all be equipped in different areas, such as assurance (1 John 3:24), boldness (Acts 4:31), expectancy (Mark 11:24), hearing Jesus' voice (John 10:4), and signs and wonders (Acts 5:12).

Not all who have had a "Divine Download" appreciate its full potential, and some people do not know how to relate the experience to their everyday lives. But for those who do, the possibilities can seem endless! We may still face many problems, and the enemy especially seems to hate it when the Spirit moves in power. But when we are under attack, or are up against it, is a good time to ask the Lord to refill us and recharge our batteries. We may need also to request this each morning, when taking on a fresh task, or when we are spiritually dry.

Who Can Be Filled? *You* Can

Just as the apostle Paul's instruction to eagerly desire the spiritual gifts was addressed to *all* the Christians at Corinth (1 Corinthians 14:1), so his injunction to be filled with the Spirit was given to *all* the church at Ephesus—not just the pastors and deacons (Ephesians 5:18). If you are a born-again Christian, you may not be particularly holy or experienced, but if you are willing and thirsty Jesus is willing to fill you with His Spirit (John 7:37–39).

In fact, the early Church recognised that all new Christians needed Spirit-baptism as soon as possible (Acts 8:14–17), just like water-baptism. The Baptism in the Spirit was part of the wider experience of conversion. Bible students have noted that the experience happened in different ways but was a stage in what may be called

The Sevenfold Christian Initiation Process (SCIP)

Not every new convert would experience every stage in this, but every stage was likely to be *available:*

1. *New Birth.* Though after responding to the Gospel water-baptism was usually considered necessary for the new Christian, the only absolute essential was new birth. It's all the dying thief had time for, but he was saved (Luke 23:43).

2. *Water Baptism.* In a generally non-Christian world, and one where believers might be persecuted, this was a shining witness to their faith.

3. *Laying-on-of-Hands* (Acts 8:15–19). It's not essential to have hands laid on you for you to receive the Holy Spirit, but this was often the way it happened, and can still.

4. *Baptism in the Spirit.* The new convert was filled with "power from on high" (Luke 24:49). It was a definite, conscious experience equipping him or her to serve Christ.

5. *Speaking in tongues* (Acts 10:44–46). This was the usual manifest sign that showed the genuineness of the new believer's regeneration and subsequent empowering by the Spirit.

6. *Joining the Church.* A natural consequence was that the new Christian joined the local assembly: for worship, fellowship, discipleship, ministry, and evangelism.

7. *Receiving Communion.* All over the world are signs of where Christians through the ages have together remembered Jesus and His death in the sacrament.

In mediaeval times, the Mass became prominent in the Church, and the Church did indeed "skip" those "Holy Spirit stages" in the initiation process. Later on an attempt was made to remedy this in those denominations which offered infant baptism. Confirmation provided an opportunity for those who had been christened as children, when they grew old enough, publicly to express their commitment to Christ. But Confirmation was also seen as an enactment of receiving the Holy Spirit through the laying-on-of-hands by the chief pastor (Acts 8:14–17). However, no manifestation of the Spirit was usually expected at this, nor was it given. Then during the Charismatic Renewal a number of Christian young people who had been taught about these things were praying to be consciously filled with the Holy Spirit and expecting God to give each of them the ability to speak in tongues. And during their

Confirmation services, as hands were laid on them, that's exactly what He did!

If you wish to have the same experience, with the right motive of getting empowered and equipped to serve the Lord more effectively, you do not have to wait for a church service! You can ask Him for it on your own, or you may wish to ask someone who has had the same experience to lay hands on you and minister it to you (Acts 19:6). If you are thirsty for God, you may find it happens to you while you are washing the dishes or mowing the lawn. But some Christians have to persevere in praying, trusting, and speaking a while before they are fluent in tongues, which is usually "part of the package."

As we continue to ask God for fresh fillings there may not be an accompanying manifestation as in the initial baptism, but it can be helpful to pray in tongues and so be edified (1 Corinthians 14:4).

The Spirit's Missing Works and Ways

Church leaders who ignore or avoid these things may do so because they are content with a different theology of the Holy Spirit that they learned at college—perhaps another legacy of cessationism. Others resent what they see as the prominence given to the gift of tongues, and fear that it might lead to division. Yet others of the younger generations may simply be unaware of what we rediscovered, and it's just not in their radar.

Consequently many fellowships largely miss out on three of the Spirit's works and three of His ways.

His Works

His filling (Ephesians 5:18 again). We have seen how this can equip us for His service.

His anointing (Luke 4:18). This is especially when the Holy Spirit anoints Christians to do particular things, such as manifesting a particular gift. But it's sometimes given to confirm the rightness of something, or simply to bring assurance. Chris especially has physical anointings—perhaps sudden surges of power onto or into her body. These can either be the Lord's way of guiding us or as a witness to those around us. If churches sing, "Breathe on me, Breath of God," they may be surprised if He does it tangibly. But this is what's happened in some gatherings when we've seen and felt Him moving among us.

Once I was leading a "Breath" residential conference at High Leigh, Hoddesdon, Hertfordshire. In the middle of a question session we suddenly sensed the Holy Spirit moving in the large hall, anointing us all. Immediately everyone's eyes were on the Lord. As I looked around, some people were praising the Lord with hands raised, some were praying in tongues, and others were receiving prayer ministry. Some were resting in the Spirit on the floor, some were talking excitedly, and others were hugging one another. The Presence of the Lord enveloped us all.

In 2 Chronicles 5:13–14, God's cloud of shekinah glory filled the Temple, overwhelming the priests and preventing them from standing up to perform their customary service. In the twenty-first century, some congregations have seen the cloud above them, hovering over certain people and bypassing others. Some the cloud overshadowed reported feeling conviction of sin. There were also instant healings and answered prayers.

His gifting (1 Corinthians 12–14). In chapter 9 of this investigation, we saw how what Paul calls spiritual gifts operate like a postal service, aiding the worship and witness of the Church.

His Ways

Supernaturally. God is able to do anything that's in accord with His righteous will and character. So it would be absolutely incredible if He ceased to work supernaturally nearly 2,000 years ago and worked only through natural means since. Yet many preachers refer *only* to the Spirit's working supernaturally in Bible times, through either ignorance, unbelief, or fear. Our God is much bigger than that!

Visibly. Much of the Spirit's work is quiet and unseen, but demonstrations of the Spirit are usually seen, to act as evidence of what God is doing (1 Corinthians 2:4). Instant miraculous healings come into this category. Ever since Jesus crossed with the Pharisees (Luke 13:14), the chief critics of the healing ministry have always been religious leaders rather than medical doctors. But praise God for the many church leaders who have discovered the value of the visible healing ministry and been blessed by including it in their church's programmes.

Suddenly. Joel Osteen, senior pastor of Lakewood, largest church in the USA (about 50,000), preached on TV on "The God of the suddenlies". The Bible speaks of many of these, not least of Christ's sudden return.

The Overflow

Between the first Easter Sunday and Pentecost, Jesus' disciples did not preach, heal or cast out demons. Peter simply went back to his old job of fishing (John 21:3). This was because they were *born* of the Spirit but not yet *baptised* in the Spirit. What a difference when Pentecost arrived! Nothing could stop them then!

After the Spirit came at Pentecost Jesus' disciples did not need to be told again to preach, heal and cast out demons, because they couldn't help doing it. They simply got on with the job. Peter and John summed it up: "We cannot help speaking about what we have seen and heard" (Acts 4:20). They *overflowed.*

What Paul calls the manifestation of the Spirit (1 Corinthians 12:7) is a part of what Jesus calls the overflow:

> If anyone is thirsty, let him come to me and drink. Whoever believes in Me, as the Scripture has said, streams of Living Water will flow from within Him (KJV: out of his belly). By this He meant the Spirit. (John 7:37–39)

What can happen when we are consciously filled with the Spirit is that His power, which may till then reside in our spirit, breaks through into our souls and bodies, bones and blood and heart and brain, and from there it flows out into the world around us, sometimes through our hands (Mark 16:18) and particularly through our mouths (Acts 1:8).

Both Jesus and Paul speak of *drinking* from the Spirit:

- "If anyone is thirsty, let him come to Me and drink .... By this He meant the Spirit" (John 7:37 and 39).
- "We were all given the one Spirit to drink" (1 Corinthians 12:13).

What's the first thing you have to do if you drink? Open your mouth.

The Bath

Another simple picture also describes what happens when we are baptised in the Holy Spirit. The unbeliever is like an empty bath. He may have lots going for him, but he is not a temple of the Holy Spirit indwelling him (1 Corinthians 6:19) and has no spiritual life (John 3:36). The born-again Christian is like a bath that has some water in, for the Holy Spirit indwells him (Romans 8:9), and the power of the Spirit is ready to be ignited. The Spirit-filled believer is like a bath filled to the brim with hot water, fully equipped and empowered to serve the Lord effectively in the immediate future. When the Christian is baptised in the Spirit he is like a bath *overflowing* with water. At the top of the bath is a little thing called the overflow, through which water escapes when it has nowhere else to go. At the top of our bodies God has put a little overflow, our mouths. Perhaps the King James Version best puts how Spirit-filled people overflow: "Then Philip opened his mouth" (Acts 8:35); "Then Peter opened his mouth" (Acts 10:34).

Continuing the analogy of the bath, when the water reaches maximum level it automatically overflows. But the bath cannot fill or refill itself—that's a human activity. In the same way a basic principle of the Holy Spirit's fullness is, "The overflow is automatic but the filling is not." If it happened automatically, why would Paul write, "Keep getting filled"? That is a *command*, for outreach and other service.

Some Christians assume that because they are now *indwelt* by the Spirit they are automatically *filled* with the Spirit's power. But they may keep this locked up inside them. It needs to be *released,* through prayer and by opening their mouths.

Spiritual Ignition

Some while ago I went to the dentist, and, after the treatment, I attempted to pay by visa card, but this was not approved. Puzzled, I paid by another method. Soon afterwards I discovered that the card had not been activated. It was a simple matter to visit a cash point machine and get the card activated. Then the money automatically flowed. Activate the Spirit's power!

A different simple illustration reveals the same thing. If you drive a car and you fill up the petrol tank, unless you then turn the ignition key, you are not going anywhere! The big open secret of successful outreach is only effective when we play our part—whether we think of us as releasing the power, activating it, or igniting the dynamite inside us.

We have now fully explored the outreach commands of Christ (Mark 16:15 and Matthew 10:7–8), and I have sought to show that they are all valuable and necessary, both for evangelism and for building up the Church. We have seen especially that Christ is expecting His Church to *preach* the full Gospel and *heal* the whole person.

Jesus is looking for ordinary people who will tell others about Him, and who are prepared to do *ex*traordinary things and give all the glory to God. What a privilege!

A Hymn about Wholeness through Christ

This may be sung, if desired, to "Moscow",
tune of *Thou Whose Almighty Word.*

That love that Jesus had

That love that Jesus had,
That love for good and bad
He gives us here.
Let's share it round today,
Let's care for those who stray,
Let's dare to show the Way
And not to fear.

"Heal the sick, win the lost
Whatever is the cost,"
He tells us now.
The deaf, the dumb, the blind,
The lame, the sick in mind,
All can in Jesus find
A Friend they know.

Let us the hungry feed,
The poor find what they need,
Sinners be won.
An invitation laid,
A demonstration weighed,
A proclamation made
Of God the Son.

Jesus we praise Your Name,
For You are still the same.
You we adore.
Wonderful Counsellor,
Saviour, Deliverer,
Healer and Conqueror,
God evermore!

John Huggett, 1983

RECOMMENDATIONS

What an inspiring book! John has truly hit the nail on the head in all he has written. Well researched biblical, historical and contemporary evidence come together to create much needed introduction and instruction for today's Christian and non-Christian alike. It is full of wise and practical advice and encouragement amassed from a treasure of long personal experience of seeing God at work powerfully in countless different situations. John's book is readable, informative and motivational and should be read by anyone with either the least or the most interest in spiritual matters — both will hugely benefit from it.

The Rev. Chris Oldroyd, ReSource Minister,
ReSource, Anglican Renewal Ministries.

The author looks back to the Charismatic Movement, 1960s to 1990s. So many gifts of the Holy Spirit were in evidence, so many healings in the Name of Jesus. But John laments that, thirty years on, "the embers have turned black", to use a memorable phrase of Michael Green. Where is the fervour? Where are the miracles? He calls the Church back to Christ's commission to preach and heal in the power of the Spirit. Much here is devoted to expounding Matthew 10:7-8, from which John gives valuable guidance on practising healing and deliverance ministries. One cannot fail to be moved by his testimony to God's supernatural power and his challenge to us to be channels to people in need.

The Rev. Dr. Andrew Daunton-Fear, Faculty, St Andrew's
Theological Seminary, Manila, Philippines, 2003-2015. Author
of "Healing in the Early Church" (Paternoster, 2009).

The book's subtitle *What does Jesus expect His Church to do?* should spur us to greater witnessing, especially through healing. "Healing ministry is still one of the best points of contact for evangelism." John shows in his investigation that God has worked supernaturally since the founding of the Church. His own extensive healing ministry qualifies him to teach us about healing and the actions of the gifts of the Holy Spirit. He gives much detailed evidence backed up by scriptural references.

Doctor Andrew Gibson, retired medical practitioner.

Printed and bound by CPI Group (UK) Ltd, Croydon, CR0 4YY